DOPAMINE DETOX

The ultimate guide to reset your brain...

OUTLINE

ABOUT THE AUTHOR

The author is a professional youtuber, content creator and author who has been featured in more than 100's of articles world wide. He has worked with influencers and content creators with over millions of followers, one of which is Kingcarlx with 4.1 million followers on tiktok.

Ever since he was a kid, he was always addicted to something and that is where his dopamine addiction occurred.

Sources of dopamine includes: Fast food, drugs, sex, alchol, netflix, your phone, social media, pornagraphy, video games and much more.

Blake Rabizadeh struggled with most of these dopamine habits and that's why he has decided to create this e-book as an ultimate guide to reset your brain.

When he quit his dopamine addiction, he was able to get a graphic design job, the small things in life like taking walks and talking with friends now brought him happiness because his brain was not constantly stimulated by intense dopamine activities like social media or video games. Enjoy!

PREFACE

The current extended work from home scenario has left the corporate world with some mixed feelings.

The virtual routines are creating roadblocks to a more productive mental health and thus overall productivity. The easy access to social media and literally virtual social existence is constantly keeping the mind engaged, robbing it away from the "flow state", thus keeping one away from being energized and hyper-focused. This often results in distraction from goals and boredom or loss of enthusiasm in work routines.

This e-book provides an insightful understanding of how mental health is a play of hormones such as dopamine, and can be reset to more constructive routines through a highly talked about silicon valley term, "the dopamine detox". The hacks and concepts shared in this book will help people experience healthy work routines and enable them to regain work enthusiasm and creativity.

INTRODUCTION

In a brain that people love to describe as "awash with chemicals," one chemical always seems to stand out. Dopamine: the molecule behind all our most sinful behaviors and secret cravings. Dopamine is love. Dopamine is lust. Dopamine is adultery. Dopamine is motivation. Dopamine is attention. Dopamine is feminism. Dopamine is addiction.

So, is dopamine your cupcake addiction? Your gambling? Your alcoholism? Your sex life? The reality is dopamine has something to do with all of these. But it is none of them. Dopamine is a chemical in your body. That's all. But that doesn't make it simple.

What is dopamine? Dopamine is one of the chemical signals that pass information from one neuron to the next in the tiny spaces between them. When it is released from the first neuron, it floats into the space (the synapse) between the two neurons, and it bumps against receptors for it on the other side that then send a signal down the receiving neuron. That sounds very simple, but when you scale it up from a single pair of neurons to the vast networks in your brain, it quickly becomes complex. The effects of dopamine release depend on where it's coming from, where the receiving neurons are going and what type of neurons they are, what receptors are binding the dopamine (there are five known types), and what role both the releasing and receiving neurons are playing.

Some people's dopamine is been busy! It's involved in many different important pathways. But when most people talk about dopamine, particularly when they talk about motivation, addiction, attention, or lust, they are talking about the dopamine pathway known as the mesolimbic pathway, which starts with cells in the ventral tegmental area, buried deep in the middle of the brain, which send their projections out to places like the nucleus accumbens and the cortex. Increases in dopamine release in the nucleus accumbens occur in response to sex, drugs, and rock and roll. And dopamine signaling in this area is changed during the course of drug addiction. All abused drugs, from alcohol to cocaine to heroin, increase dopamine in this area in one way or another, and many people like to describe a spike in dopamine as "motivation" or "pleasure." But that's not quite it. Really, dopamine is signaling feedback for predicted rewards. If you, say, have learned to associate a cue (like a crack pipe) with a hit of crack, you will start getting increases in dopamine in the nucleus accumbens in response to the sight of the pipe, as your brain predicts the reward. But if you then don't get your hit, well, then dopamine can decrease, and that's not a good feeling. So you'd think that maybe dopamine predicts reward. But again, it gets more complex. For example, dopamine can increase in the nucleus accumbens in people with post-traumatic stress disorder when they are experiencing heightened vigilance and paranoia. So you might say, in this brain area at least, dopamine isn't addiction or reward or fear. Instead, it's what we call salience. Salience is more than attention: It's a sign of something that needs to be paid attention to, something that stands out. This may be part of the mesolimbic role in attention deficit hyperactivity disorder and also a part of its role in addiction.

But dopamine itself? It's not salience. It has far more roles in the brain to play. For example, dopamine plays a big role in starting movement, and the destruction of dopamine neurons in an area of the brain called the substantia nigra is what produces the symptoms of Parkinson's disease. Dopamine also plays an important role as a hormone, inhibiting prolactin to stop the release of breast milk. Back in the mesolimbic pathway, dopamine can play a role in psychosis, and many antipsychotics for treatment of schizophrenia target dopamine. Dopamine is involved in the frontal cortex in executive functions like attention. In the rest of the body, dopamine is involved in nausea, in kidney function, and in heart function.

With all of these wonderful, interesting things that dopamine does, it gets to me to see dopamine simplified to things like "attention" or "addiction." After all, it's so easy to say "dopamine is X" and call it a day. It's comforting. You feel like you know the truth at some fundamental biological level, and that's that. And there are always enough studies out there showing the role of dopamine in X to leave you convinced. But simplifying dopamine, or any chemical in the brain, down to a single action or result gives people a false picture of what it is and what it does. If you think that dopamine is motivation, then more must be better, right? Not necessarily! Because if dopamine is also "pleasure" or "high," then too much is far too much of a good thing. If you think of dopamine as only being about pleasure or only being about attention, you'll end up with a false idea of some of the problems involving dopamine, like drug addiction or attention deficit hyperactivity disorder, and you'll end up with false ideas of how to fix them.

If you believe "dopamine is," then you'd think that we've got it all figured out. You begin to wonder why we haven't solved this addiction problem yet. Complexity means that the diseases associated with dopamine (or with any other chemical or part of the brain, for that matter) are often difficult to understand and even more difficult to treat.

By emphasizing dopamine's complexity, it might feel like I'm taking away some of the glamour, the sexiness, of dopamine. But I don't think so. The complexity of how a neurotransmitter behaves is what makes it wonderful. The simplicity of a single molecule and its receptors is what makes dopamine so flexible and what allows the resulting systems to be so complex. And it's not just dopamine. While dopamine has just five receptor type, another neurotransmitter, serotonin, has 14 currently known and even more that are thought to exist. Other neurotransmitters have receptors with different subtypes, all expressed in different places, and where each combination can produce a different result. There are many types of neurons, and they make billions and billions of connections. And all of this so you can walk, talk, eat, fall in love, get married, get divorced, get addicted to cocaine, and come out on top of your addiction some day. When you think of the sheer number of connections required simply for you to read and understand this sentence—from eyes to brain, to processing, to understanding, to movement as your fingers scroll down the page—you begin to feel a sense of awe. Our brain does all this, even while it makes us think about pepperoni pizza and what that text your crush sent really means. Complexity makes the brain the fascinating and mind-boggling thing that it is.

So, dopamine has to do with addiction, whether to cupcakes or cocaine. It has to do with lust and love. It has to do with milk. It has to do with movement, motivation, attention, psychosis. Dopamine plays a role in all of these. But it is none of them, and we shouldn't want it to be. Its complexity is what makes it great. It shows us what, with a single molecule, the brain can do.

ALL ABOUT DOPAMINE

Dopamine, like all neurochemicals, is involved in many processes throughout the brain and body. It is most notoriously implicated in drug addiction, which led people to believe that dopamine was a pleasure chemical. But in fact, scientists see the biggest dopamine surge in anticipation of a reward, not in response to one. Researchers now believe that dopamine is a salient signal telling the brain what to pay attention to. This fits with one of the neurochemical's other important roles: facilitating learning. Dopamine teaches the brain to repeat a behavior or experience that was pleasurable or beneficial, but it doesn't contribute to the feeling of pleasure itself.

Evolutionarily, it is meant to act as a means of positive re-enforcement – but in the modern age of instant gratification and cheap excess, constantly chasing a dopamine high has become a hindrance to people's development and life goals.

It is responsible for that amazing feeling we get when we accomplish something good. The flip-side is that it's also responsible for many of our really bad habits and time-wasting pursuits.

Dopamine is a neurotransmitter that plays several important roles in the brain and body. It is an organic chemical of the catecholamine and phenethylamine families. Dopamine constitutes about 80% of the catecholamine content in the brain. It is an amine synthesized by removing a carboxyl group from a molecule of its precursor chemical, L-DOPA, which is synthesized in the brain and kidneys. Dopamine is also synthesized in plants and most animals. In the brain, dopamine functions as a neurotransmitter—a chemical released by neurons (nerve cells) to send signals to other nerve cells. Neurotransmitters are synthesized in specific regions of the brain, but affect many regions systemically. The brain includes several distinct dopamine pathways, one of which plays a major role in the motivational component of reward-motivated behavior. The anticipation of most types of rewards increases the level of dopamine in the brain, and many addictive drugs increase dopamine release or block its reuptake into neurons following release. Other brain dopamine pathways are involved in motor control and in controlling the release of various hormones. These pathways and cell groups form a dopamine system which is neuromodulatory.

Dopamine which is a type of neurotransmitter in the brain is naturally produced by the body as a chemical messenger, and it affects many behavioral and physical functions, including:

• learning

• motivation

• sleep

• mood

• attention

An excess or deficiency in dopamine production can cause mental health conditions. Exposure to overwhelming levels of stimuli can prompt such disorders, leading to dependencies on certain substances or activities.

In popular culture and media, dopamine is usually seen as the main chemical of pleasure, but the current opinion in pharmacology is that dopamine instead confers motivational salience; in other words, dopamine signals the perceived motivational prominence (i.e., the desirability or aversiveness) of an outcome, which in turn propels the organism's behavior toward or away from achieving that outcome.

Outside the central nervous system, dopamine functions primarily as a local paracrine messenger. In blood vessels, it inhibits norepinephrine release and acts as a vasodilator (at normal concentrations); in the kidneys, it increases sodium excretion and urine output; in the pancreas, it reduces insulin production; in the digestive system, it reduces gastrointestinal motility and protects intestinal mucosa; and in the immune system, it reduces the activity of lymphocytes. With the exception of the blood vessels, dopamine in each of these peripheral systems is synthesized locally and exerts its effects near the cells that release it.

Several important diseases of the nervous system are associated with dysfunctions of the dopamine system, and some of the key medications used to treat them work by altering the effects of dopamine. Parkinson's disease, a degenerative condition causing tremor and motor impairment, is caused by a loss of dopamine-secreting neurons in an area of the midbrain called the substantia nigra. Its metabolic precursor L-DOPA can be manufactured; Levodopa, a pure form of L-DOPA, is the most widely used treatment for Parkinson's. There is evidence that schizophrenia involves altered levels of dopamine activity, and most antipsychotic drugs used to treat this are dopamine antagonists which reduce dopamine activity. Similar dopamine antagonist drugs are also some of the most effective anti-nausea agents. Restless legs syndrome and attention deficit hyperactivity disorder (ADHD) are associated with decreased dopamine activity. Dopaminergic stimulants can be addictive in high doses, but some are used at lower doses to treat ADHD. Dopamine itself is available as a manufactured medication for intravenous injection: although it cannot reach the brain from the bloodstream, its peripheral effects make it useful in the treatment of heart failure or shock, especially in newborn babies.

What do drug addiction and Parkinson's disease have in common? Improper levels of dopamine (DOAP-uh-meen). This chemical acts as a messenger between brain cells. Dopamine is important for many of our daily behaviors. It plays a role in how we move, for instance, as well as what we eat, how we learn and even whether we become addicted to drugs.

They shuttle across the spaces between cells. These messengers then bind to docking-station molecules called receptors. Those receptors relay the signal carried by the neurotransmitter from one cell to its neighbor.

Different neurotransmitters are made in different parts of the brain. Two main brain areas produce dopamine. One is called the substantia nigra (Sub-STAN-sha NY-grah). It's a tiny strip of tissue on either side of the base of your brain. It sits in a region known as the midbrain. Close by is the ventral tegmental area. It, too, makes dopamine.

These two brain areas are very thin and tiny. Together they are smaller than a postage stamp. But the dopamine they produce relays signals that travel throughout the brain. Dopamine from the substantia nigra helps us begin movements and speech. When the brain cells that make dopamine in this area start to die off, a person can have trouble initiating movement. It's just one of the many symptoms ravaging people with Parkinson's disease (a condition best known for uncontrollable tremors). To move normally, patients with Parkinson's take a drug that lets them make more dopamine (or they get an implant that stimulates deep regions of the brain).

The dopamine from the ventral tegmental area doesn't help people move — at least, not directly. Instead, this area usually sends dopamine into the brain when animals (including people) expect or receive a reward. That reward might be a delicious slice of pizza or a favorite song. This dopamine release tells the brain that whatever it just experienced is worth getting more of. And that helps animals (including people) change their behaviors in ways that will help them attain more of the rewarding item or experience.

Dopamine also helps with reinforcement — motivating an animal to do something again and again. Dopamine is what prompts a lab animal, for instance, to repeatedly press a lever to get tasty pellets of food. And it's part of why humans seek out another slice of pizza. Reward and reinforcement help us learn where to find important things such as food or water, so that we can go back for more. Dopamine even affects moods. Things that are rewarding tend to make us feel pretty good. Lowering dopamine can make animals lose pleasure in activities like eating and drinking. This joyless state is called anhedonia.

Because of its roles in reward and reinforcement, dopamine also helps animals focus on things. Anything that's rewarding, after all, is usually well worth our attention.

But dopamine has a more sinister side. Drugs such as cocaine, nicotine and heroin cause huge boosts in dopamine. The "high" people feel when they use drugs comes partly from that dopamine spike. And that prompts people to seek out those drugs again and again — even though they are harmful. Indeed, the brain "reward" associated with that high can lead to drug abuse and eventually to addiction.

HOW DO WE MAKE DOPAMINE?

In the modern world, many stimuli provide quick and sustained dopamine hits. Smartphone usage, playing video games excessively, obsessions with pornography, and social media are just a few of the most common highs that we chase.

Natural neurotransmitter release from pleasurable activities like eating a delicious meal is strongest when we first engage in the activity but will tend to wane the longer it goes on. At some point we are full, and we want to find another source of stimulation.

However, modern addictive activities like those previously mentioned introduce new stimuli consistently, which keeps us hooked without ever wanting to do something new. Our brains are tricked into thinking that we are doing something good and meaningful.

WHAT DOES DOPAMINE DO?

Dopamine is implicated in feelings of pleasure and plays a prominent role in addiction. People with substance dependencies may grow dependent partially because of the activation of dopamine. Some other ways dopamine affects the body include:

Mood regulation: Insufficient dopamine can contribute to depression. Meanwhile, some research has found that too much dopamine could cause mania.

Slows the production of prolactin: Prolactin is involved in both lactation and sexual gratification.

Regulates sleep: Dopamine helps inhibit the production of melatonin toward the end of a night's sleep, contributing to wakefulness.

Regulates attention and memory: Many studies have demonstrated dopamine's link to attention, memory, and cognition. Disruptions in dopamine have been connected to attention-deficit hyperactivity (ADHD) and schizophrenia, for example.

Increases goal-oriented behavior: In addition to promoting reward and goal-driven behavior, dopamine may decrease inhibition.

Irregular dopamine levels can cause a variety of psychological problems. For instance, Parkinson's disease is caused partially by the death of dopamine-secreting neurons. Drugs that increase dopamine production may help people with Parkinson's, particularly during the early stages of the disease.

HOW TO INCREASE DOPAMINE

There are a wide variety of activities that boost dopamine levels in the brain, but not all of them contribute to long-term health. Taking part in behaviors that increase dopamine while improving your health can contribute to the formation of good habits and boost your mood. Some ways to get a natural increase in dopamine include:

Consume probiotics: Whether taken in supplement form or by eating probiotic rich foods such as yogurt and fermented foods, probiotics have been shown to support dopamine production.

Sleep: Getting enough sleep each night is one of the best ways to keep your dopamine at a healthy level. One night without sleep has actually been shown to increase dopamine in the short-term. However, the increase in dopamine caused by long-term sleep deprivation could cause dopamine receptors to become less sensitive to dopamine, making it difficult for a person to feel awake.

Spend time in the sun: Sunlight facilitates the body's production of vitamin D. Vitamin D, in turn, can help increase dopamine production.

Exercise: In addition to endorphins, exercise can increase dopamine levels, contributing to the mood improvement that often comes with physical activity.

Listen to music: Multiple studies have shown that listening to music you like causes dopamine to be released in the brain.

Avoid sugary foods and junk food: Eating foods that release large amounts of dopamine (which are often high in sugar and fat) can have a desensitizing effect over time. Sticking to whole foods ensures the body's dopamine receptors don't become overpowered, thereby creating the need for foods that stimulate the release of more dopamine.

DOPAMINE AND ADDICTION

Dopamine is well-known for the role it plays in addiction. As it plays a key role in helping develop habits that support health and survival, so can it support the formation of self-destructive coping mechanisms.

Whether the addiction is to sugary food, sex, alcohol, or drugs, the role dopamine plays is the same. Addictive substances overload the brain with dopamine, causing dopamine receptors to become less sensitive to it. Higher and higher amounts of dopamine are then required in order to get the same initial feeling caused by the addictive substance. When the addictive substance is not delivered in higher amounts or withheld completely, withdrawal symptoms may appear.

Researchers have found that dopamine plays a similar role in many compulsive behaviors, such as compulsive pornography use, internet addiction, and compulsive gambling. These behaviors stimulate a similar rush of dopamine to the brain, establishing it as rewarding and reinforcing it as a habit. Individuals with these compulsions may feel as though they have lost control over that aspect of their behavior.

DOPAMINE AND MENTAL HEALTH

Dopamine also has significant function in some mental health conditions. A few of these include:

Schizophrenia: Dopamine dysregulation has been found to be present in the brains of individuals with schizophrenia. It may be at least partly responsible for both positive and negative symptoms of schizophrenia, including hallucinations and delusions as well as a lack of pleasure and motivation.

Depression: While depression is classically associated more often with serotonin dysregulation, some research supports the idea that dopamine could also be associated with the loss of pleasure, or anhedonia, associated with depression.

ADHD: Dopamine is thought to be a key factor in the development of ADHD. Studies have shown that lower than usual amounts of dopamine in the brain are often present alongside symptoms of ADHD.

Anxiety: One study linked anxiety to insufficient dopamine in the amygdala. Since the amygdala is implicated in the fight or flight response, dopamine could act as a way to quiet the amygdala when it reacts to a "false alarm." Without enough dopamine to stop the fight or flight response, higher levels of anxiety could be the result.

Research exploring the many links between dopamine and mental health is ongoing, and experts are still discovering all the ways dopamine is connected to behavioral health.

It's also possible to have too much dopamine. Effects of overly high dopamine levels include high libido, anxiety, difficulty sleeping, increased energy, mania, stress, and improved ability to focus and learn, among others. When certain parts of the brain are exposed to too much dopamine, for instance right after an individual takes illicit drugs, other behaviors may be present. These can include aggression, hallucinations, twitching, nausea and/or vomiting, and depression.

DOPAMINE AND PSYCHOACTIVE DRUGS

Because dopamine contributes to feelings of pleasure, a rush of dopamine can cause an immediate change in mood. Dopamine-producing drugs such as Adderall and Dexadrine are sometimes prescribed to people experiencing treatment-resistant depression. Medications that increase dopamine production can be highly addictive, and thus are not recommended for people with substance abuse problems. Some dopamine-producing drugs can also cause cardiovascular and renal problems, and people prescribed amphetamines and related drugs should be carefully monitored by a physician.

WHAT IF I HAVE TOO LITTLE OR TOO MUCH DOPAMINE?

Dopamine dysregulation could mean that the brain is producing too little or too much dopamine. Low dopamine, or dopamine deficiency, can be caused by a variety of factors, including conditions such as Parkinson's disease, schizophrenia, and depression. Drug and sugar addiction have also been found to cause dopamine deficiency over time. Some low dopamine symptoms include fatigue, moodiness, dysphoria, physical pain, and changes in weight, sex drive, and ability to focus. As many other conditions share these symptoms, it's important to consult your health care provider if you're experiencing these symptoms. Things that you once enjoyed are no longer exciting when compared to the new addictive activities that you are pursuing.

Here's the thing, our brains can't tell the difference between a source of dopamine that is from a productive reward and one that from a time-wasting reward. To our brains, they are both the same.

Human nature being what it is, we are far more likely to chase after the easier and more potent of the two types of activities. Why spend time building a business or working on a relationship when you can just hop online for a quick fix?

We end up wasting time doing things we know that we should not by chasing chemical highs. We literally become addicted to the devices and behaviors that enable them.

So… what's the solution?

Initiating a factory reset.

Simply, we need to reset our brains. By reducing the frequency in which we engage in these damaging behaviors, we can retrain our brains to recognize NORMAL levels of dopamine stimulation. Doing so will increase the number of dopamine neuroreceptors in a process called up-regulation – the result is that we will be more sensitive to natural levels of stimulation.

We can return to enjoying things that we used to without the excessive craving for more.

The concept of dopamine fasting which we shall be considering next is incredibly simple, but in practice, it can be extremely challenging.

DOPAMINE FASTING

This might sound strange to you, but do you know that dopamine fasting is the only fast that does not include dieting! How exciting does it sound? To keep it more simple, dopamine fasting is a new kind of fast wherein you don't have to give up your favorite foods. The aim is to abstain from pleasurable activities.

Now, the question arises here, how are you going to do it? Dopamine levels can reset with the help of abstaining from things or stuff that brings you pleasure like social media, smartphones, foods, eye-contact, Netflix, video games, and more.

Dopamine fasting is the newest type of fasting that has nothing to do with diet. With the help of Dopamine Fasting, people generally abstain from pleasurable interactions that could change dopamine levels in the brain.

The whole idea behind the concept of "Dopamine Fasting" is to address compulsive behaviors that interfere with your happiness. Dopamine Fasting helps in controlling the dominance of technology in the day to day life. The other benefit of Dopamine Fasting is that you can expect fewer notifications, beeps, and rings.

Some people related "dopamine fasting" with the Silicon Valley concept. The idea was to make people understand about resetting dopamine receptors.

It's the latest wellness trend direct from Silicon Valley in the States but what exactly is this new fad and does it actually work?

Dopamine fasting is a form of digital detox, involving temporarily abstaining from addictive technologies such as social media, listening to music on technological platforms, and Internet gaming, and can be extended to temporary deprivation of social interaction and eating. The term's origins are unknown; it was first widely promoted by the life coach "Improvement Pill" in November 2018 on YouTube.

The practice has been referred to as a "maladaptive fad" by Harvard researchers. Other critics say that it is based on a misunderstanding of how the neurotransmitter dopamine, which operates within the brain to reward behavior, actually works and can be altered by conscious behavior.

The idea behind it is to take a break from the repetitive patterns of excitement and stimulation that can be triggered by interaction with digital technology, and that the practice of avoiding pleasurable activities can work to undo bad habits, allow time for self-reflection, and bolster personal happiness.

The practice of dopamine fasting is not clearly defined in what it entails, on what technologies, with what frequency it should be done, or how it is supposed to work. Some proponents limit the process to avoiding online technology; others extend it to abstaining from all work, exercise, physical contact and unnecessary conversation.

According to Cameron Sepah, a proponent of the practice, the purpose is not to literally reduce dopamine in the body but rather to reduce impulsive behaviors that are rewarded by it. One account suggests that the practice is about avoiding cues, such as hearing the ring of a smartphone, that can trigger impulsive behaviors, such as remaining on the smartphone after the call to play a game.[10] In one sense, dopamine fasting is a reaction to technology firms which have engineered their services to keep people hooked.

Dopamine fasting has been said to resemble the fasting tradition of many religions. An extreme form of dopamine fasting would be complete sensory deprivation, where all external stimuli are removed in order to promote a sense of calm and wellbeing.

The idea of dopamine fasting originated in – where else – Silicon Valley. Yes, the place that has spent years carefully engineering and designing their products and apps to exploit the dopamine system and get us hooked has now decided that overloading our brains with this chemical might not be such a good idea after all. Some think we're so overstimulated by things like social media, TV and the internet, that we've become desensitised to pleasure.

The answer? An enforced break from doing anything that triggers dopamine to 'reset' our brains and allow us to appreciate the simple things again. This isn't your bog standard digital detox. Avid dopamine fasters cut out all stimulating and pleasurable activities from their lives – eating, entertainment, exercise, screen time, even conversation – for periods of 24 hours or more. A viral New York Times piece on the trend featured a startup founder called James Sinker explaining how during a fast he 'avoid[s] eye contact because it excites me.'

Inevitably, the idea of dopamine fasting has been ripped apart by many. Experts are widely skeptical too. As Dr Ciara McCabe, Associate Professor in Neuroscience at the University of Reading explained in a piece breaking down the science of the trend, dopamine plays an important role in lots of everyday functions and it's not a good idea to try and reduce it. Also, the idea that we can somehow 'reset' our brains by avoiding dopamine triggers for a short while is 'nonsense'.

Yet get away from the extreme examples, and there are some useful ideas behind the concept. 'The general idea is that cutting back on things that you are finding problematic in your life is a good thing, of course and this makes sense,' Dr McCabe admits.

Dopamine is released in anticipation of pleasurable activities. It's the notifications that ping on our phone and make us think there might be an exciting message that trigger it, not the message itself. If we want to cut back on certain behaviours – like an addiction to social media – we need to reduce our exposure to the cues that trigger this.

'One role of dopamine is to initiate motivation to seek rewards,' says Dr McCabe. 'Dopamine activates to the signals that rewards (such as Facebook likes) are coming, like a notification sound on your smartphone. Turning off notifications is a simple way to not activate dopamine which helps to reduce the drive to constantly check your phone for rewards.'

Even Dr Cameron Sepah, pioneer of dopamine fasting, admits the name is a bit misleading. He says it's not about reducing dopamine itself but impulsive behaviours, by avoiding the stimuli that encourage our addiction to certain activities. That could be putting our phone away and using special software to stop us aimlessly surfing the internet or learning how to recognise our urges and let them pass without acting on them.

Dopamine fasting might be a fad, but the basic idea of setting boundaries and taking time away from stuff we're become hooked on and habits that aren't that good for our wellbeing makes sense. And no, you really don't have to avoid eye contact to do it.

NO ONE IS ACTUALLY FASTING FROM DOPAMINE

It's important to note that, despite the name, the original idea behind dopamine fasting is not to literally lower dopamine levels.

"The goal is not to reduce dopamine or elicit functional brain changes," Sepah, allayed. Instead, dopamine fasting encourages people to reduce the "time spent on problematic behavior," he said.

Still, research shows there is a connection between dopamine and problematic behavior, such as drug abuse.

When the brain picks up clues that it may soon receive a reward — whether that reward be food, illicit drugs or likes on social media — a flash of dopamine zaps the reward pathway, according to Slate. Another hit of dopamine comes with the reward itself. Addictive substances and behaviors repeatedly bombard the reward pathway with huge surges of dopamine, and over time, the brain morphs in response.

"When we image [drug users'] brains, we find that in the immediate aftermath of using they actually have less dopamine and fewer dopamine receptors than those who don't use drugs," said Dr. Anna Lembke, an associate professor and medical director of addiction medicine at Stanford University.

All addictive drugs cause dopamine levels to spike in one way or another, Lembke said, and in response, the brain weakens or eliminates the receptors built to respond to the chemical. That means drug users need more of the substance to elicit the same surge of dopamine, and that other rewards, like food and social interaction, steadily lose their appeal.

By any other name

As a clinician, Lembke recommends that her patients with drug addictions enter a "period of abstinence" in order to reset the brain's reward system. By its rpurest definition, a period of abstinence is not unlike a dopamine fast, in which people abstain from problematic behaviors.

"I call them detox periods," Dr. David Greenfield, an assistant clinical professor of psychiatry at the University of Connecticut School of Medicine, told Live Science. "We go through a period where we allow those receptors to calm down."

Greenfield treats a destructive behavior that may impact the Silicon Valley folks drawn to dopamine fasting:

compulsive internet and technology use. Dopamine surges in the brain's reward system each time we so much as glance at a smartphone or laptop screen, he said, and rewarding notifications and media pop up unpredictably whenever we go online. People grow addicted to devices, just as they do to drugs, Greenfield said. Lembke said she has witnessed the phenomenon, too.

"People are coming into my clinic with severe, pathological, compulsive use of these interfaces," she said. Although internet and video-game addictions have yet to be recognized as true disorders in the bible of mental health disorders, the DSM-5, experts recognize that both substance use and excessive screen time wreak similar havoc in the brain. And just like drug addiction, the goal of treatment "is to detox from the most problematic sites and content," Greenfield wrote in a 2018 article on internet and video game addiction.

But after the initial period of abstinence, the real work begins, he added.

WHERE DID THE TERM "DOPAMINE FASTING" COME FROM?

Sepah didn't invent the name "dopamine fasting." The term has been used on internet discussion forums since at least 2016. A man named Greg Kamphuis launched "The Dopamine Challenge" and took to Reddit to invite people to join him in a 40-day fast from "TV, refined sugar, alcohol, processed fats, nicotine, recreational drugs, caffeine, and porn" while also "making deliberate choices about meal times, social media, and shopping."

Kamphuis described the fast as his "desperate attempt to get healthy and motivated" and to "sacrifice a few weeks of pleasure to search for a lifetime of joy."

Right there we see a common misconception about dopamine: People often think of it as "the pleasure molecule," that thing in our brains that makes us feel good. But neuroscientists will tell you that's oversimplifying to the point of inaccuracy.

Dopamine is involved in the complex process of reward-based learning, memory, and motivation. When you find a sugary snack, eat it, and discover it tastes delicious, your brain releases dopamine, which helps lay down a context-dependent memory. It's a signal that says, "Remember what you're eating and where you found it!" Dopamine also motivates you to repeat the process — to get up and go looking for that sugary snack again in the future.

When Kamphuis circulated his idea for a dopamine fast, it didn't seem to attract broad appeal. But this August, when Sepah published his guide and taught it to Silicon Valley execs, it took off. He used the term "dopamine fasting 2.0" to differentiate the modified protocol he created, which is a lot easier than Kamphuis's. It recommends that you abstain for a short period (as short as one hour per day) from whichever specific behavior has become problematic for you — whether it's gaming, gambling, scrolling through social media, or something else.

Now, however, he says his protocol has been misinterpreted. People like Sinka, the eye-contact-avoider, are engaged in "their own extremist practice," Sepah told me, "which is completely incompatible with my protocol."

Sepah thinks the media — which he says likes to mock "Silicon Valley male excess" — is partly to blame for the misunderstanding. In a blog post, he wrote that the Times was wrong to claim that "dopamine fasting is basically a fast of everything," and that his original guide makes clear what dopamine fasting is not: an avoidance of dopamine or of anything stimulating.

It's true that the guide does not advocate fasting from social contact — in fact, it actually recommends that people talk and bond with others while they're dopamine fasting. Yet it's not surprising that some in Silicon Valley have interpreted the gospel of dopamine fasting in this way. If you don't want people to interpret a practice as an avoidance of dopamine, it's probably best not to call it dopamine fasting.

"Dopamine is just a mechanism that explains how addictions can become reinforced, and makes for a catchy title," Sepah told the Times. "The title's not to be taken literally."

But of course, once a practice makes the rounds — which it will, precisely because it's been given a catchy title — people will make of it what they will. (It's also worth noting the irony here: The title refers to a practice designed to undercut the attention economy, yet the very name was used because it grabs your attention.)

What's the scientific evidence in support of dopamine fasting?

Research says that taking a break from activities stops the turning of the dopamine system. However, it does not reset it. That does not clear up the mind. Dopamine fasting resets the dopamine receptors. When you try to reset dopamine levels through dopamine fasting, it increases the pleasure of resting. As dopamine was thought to be a pleasure neurotransmitter or chemical, however, researchers have evidence about its working more deeply.

Dopamine is basically related to motivation and is an important part when someone discusses the treatment of addictions. However, it is more complicated than this. Dopamine is related to the large rewards system in our brain. Rewards are considered for the things that we want and like.

To understand this let's take an example, whenever you hear the notification sound in your phone from a distance, you wish to see the text. This happens because the sound of notification triggered dopamine. These little things are triggers for dopamine. These small hits of dopamine are invigorating, they are distressing and distracting.

Some people have interpreted dopamine fasting as being about, well, reducing dopamine. But if that's your goal, you've got a problem, because generally speaking dopamine is not under our control.

Dopamine floods your system when you experience unanticipated things — finding chocolate where you didn't expect to find any, for example. But if something becomes expected (there's always chocolate in your office snack room at noon), then dopamine starts firing in anticipation of getting that reward. So, can somebody really fast from dopamine?

"Well, if they're anticipating anything — like eating chocolate or having a conversation — that's not something you typically have conscious control over," Judson Brewer, a neuroscientist and psychiatrist at Brown University who specializes in addiction, told me. "You can't stop anticipating something. If you see chocolate, your brain thinks, 'Oh that looks good!' You can't tell your brain, 'Hey, don't do that.'"

Brewer laughed when he heard about the Silicon Valley start-up founders who are avoiding everything from eye contact to social interactions in an attempt to avoid dopamine. "That's hilarious!" he said. "Leave it to people to take everything to an extreme and not understand how their own brains work."

But to be fair, we should distinguish this extreme interpretation from the goal Sepah actually proposed — which is not, despite the unnecessarily confusing name, to reduce dopamine.

"The point of dopamine fasting is to increase behavioral flexibility, by reducing impulsive behavior for extended periods of time," Sepah told me in an email. "By both avoiding conditioned stimuli (e.g. notifications) that trigger impulsive behavior, and also naturally exposing ourselves to unconditioned stimuli (e.g. negative feelings of anxiety, boredom, or loneliness) but not giving into a conditioned response (e.g. grabbing for our phones, or eating a sugary snack), this helps weaken that conditioning over time."

Basically, by avoiding stimuli like smartphone notifications and also exposing ourselves to uncomfortable feelings without giving in to the temptation to distract ourselves, we can break our habit of grabbing our devices anytime they ding or we feel bad.

This is classic behaviorism, and it's perfectly fine, as far as it goes. The idea that we should practice exposing ourselves to anxious, bored, or lonely feelings without resorting to our usual escape methods, like checking our phones, is one you'll find in countless CBT-based guides to distress tolerance nowadays.

Brewer said he doesn't question whether Sepah's proposal is accurately classified as CBT (it is) or whether Sepah is right to say that if we don't take breaks from overstimulating technologies, we'll seek out ever-higher doses of stimulation (that's basic habituation). However, he does question dopamine fasting as a strategy for the long haul.

"You can force yourself to fast, but that's not actually going to be useful in the long term," Brewer said. His reasoning: If you fast one day a week for the rest of your life, that's just going to deprive you of whatever you like. But because you still like it, you're going to keep coming back to it.

It's much better, Brewer says, to teach your brain that a given activity — like scrolling through social media for hours on end — is not actually very rewarding. When you realize that a behavior leaves you feeling bad, it becomes much easier to moderate it. You no longer need to force yourself to abstain; instead, abstaining is a natural byproduct of your distaste.

Sounds nice, but how do you achieve that? The answer, Brewer said, is mindfulness. Through paying close attention to an experience in real time, you can teach your brain that the experience is not truly rewarding.

Brewer's lab has shown that app-based mindfulness training — which combines awareness of the present moment with an attitude of nonjudgmental curiosity — can help smokers and overeaters reduce their unhealthy habits by as much as 40 percent.

According to Brewer, if you want to short-circuit your drive to go after more and more dopamine, "You've got to give your brain a bigger, better offer." That offer is curiosity, which feels better than a craving and is not dopamine-driven, so long as it's rooted in interest rather than deprivation (the I-need-to-find-out-right-now-or-I'm-going-to-die feeling). The best part, Brewer said, is that "intrinsically rewarding behaviors such as curiosity don't become habituated — you don't deplete curiosity."

IS DOPAMINE FASTING JUST REPACKAGING OLD IDEAS?

A perennial frustration with Silicon Valley is that it tends to come up with "trends" that it markets as innovative new discoveries when really they're centuries-old practices. Case in point: In January, Dorsey tweeted about how he feels like time slows down when he's engaged in intermittent fasting and asked, "Anyone else have this experience?" It prompted a collective eyeroll from Muslims and others who've long fasted as part of their religious observance.

Now, some people are asking what differentiates dopamine fasting from preexisting practices — Buddhist meditation retreats, say, or the Jewish Sabbath, which involves abstaining from electronic devices for a day but also involves engaging in prosocial activity. For that matter, how different is dopamine fasting from commonsense ideas like simply taking a break, enjoying a weekend, or going on vacation?

Very different, according to Sepah.

"Meditation/silent retreats involve practicing mindfulness and sometimes not speaking. Dopamine fasting involves neither," he told me. "Sabbath is focused on not working in favor of religious worship. You can absolutely work during a dopamine fast if it's values-aligned and is not a religious practice. Vacations are often treated as opportunities for unbridled hedonism and actually doing more bad habits, so it's almost the opposite of dopamine fasting."

Sepah argues that his recommended schedule for abstaining from gaming, gambling, or whichever behavior is problematic for you also makes dopamine fasting unique. Here's what he prescribes:

- 1-4 hours at the end of the day (depending on work & family demands)
- 1 weekend day (spend it outside on a Saturday or Sunday)
- 1 weekend per quarter (go on a local trip)
- 1 week per year (go on vacation!)

This sounds a lot like common sense; some of us do this already. But Sepah's point is not just that we should take a vacation but that what we do while we're on vacation matters. The vacation is just the vessel; dopamine fasting is what you fill it with. "I recommended dopamine fasting be done during nights, weekends, and vacation periods because that's realistically when people have time to practice," he clarifed.

Fair enough. It probably would be good for our health if we were more intentional about how we spend our limited free time, using it as a chance to practice things that modern life has made us extra uncomfortable with — like being alone or being bored — by offering us ubiquitous, immediate escapes in the form of digital devices.

There's nothing objectionable about this recommendation per se. The problem has more to do with the name of the practice, which practically begs to be misconstrued, and with the claim that the practice represents an ideal long-term strategy. Although Sepah says he's created "the antidote to our overstimulated age," in reality he seems to have created something more like a stopgap measure, one prone to being misinterpreted in harshly ascetic ways.

DOPAMINE FASTING 2.0: THE HOT SILICON VALLEY TREND

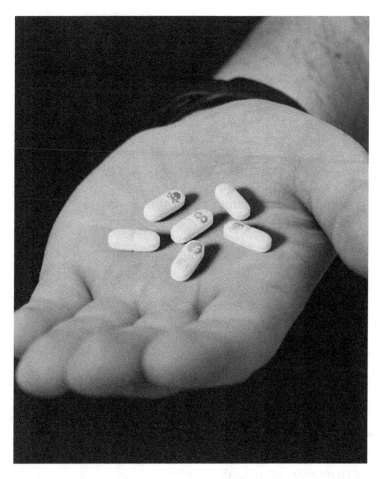

Dopamine Fasting has gone viral worldwide! This article has 140K+ views, and the international media from the ABC, The New York Times, BBC, and other prominent media have covered it across the US, UK, Australia, Finland, France, Japan, India, Russia, Turkey, and the Middle East. So what is all the rage about? Dopamine

Fasting 2.0 is an evidence-based technique to manage addictive behaviors, by restricting them to specific periods of time, and practicing fasting from impulsively engaging in them, in order to regain behavioral flexibility. Unfortunately, there's also been a lot of public misunderstanding due to media misportrayals, so let's start with what it ISN'T.

Here's what Dopamine Fasting IS NOT:

- Reducing dopamine (the focus is on reducing impulsive BEHAVIOR)

- Avoiding all stimulation/pleasure (focuses only on specific behaviors that are problematic for you)

- Not talking/socializing/exercising (actually encourages values-aligned health behaviors)

- Rebranding meditation/asceticism/sabbath (doesn't involve meditating or not working)

- Vacation (people treat vacations as times to indulge even more in bad habits)

- A "tech bro" or Silicon Valley-only trend (it's done by both genders all over the world)

What's the Science behind Dopamine Fasting 2.0?

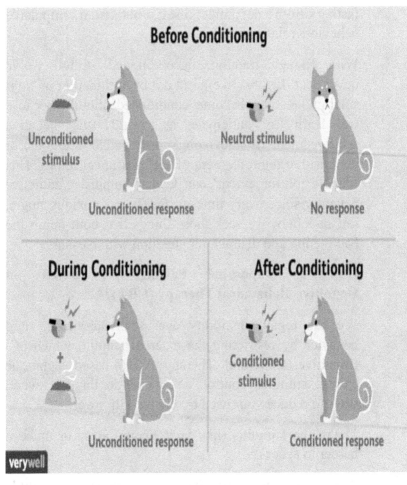

Before Conditioning

Unconditioned stimulus

Unconditioned response

Neutral stimulus

No response

During Conditioning

Unconditioned response

After Conditioning

Conditioned stimulus

Conditioned response

verywell

Let's first understand how impulsive behaviors become problematic or addictive. If you've ever studied behaviorism in a psychology course, you may recall that "classical conditioning" is a process which helps us learn that involves dopamine. To be clear, we ARE NOT fasting from dopamine itself, but from impulsive behaviors reinforced by it.

With enough training, unconditioned stimuli we've never seen before, like a red dot or notification on your smartphone, can become conditioned stimuli, because we learn to anticipate a reward (the negative reinforcement of alleviating our negative emotions, or the positive reinforcement of seeing a novel thing). This 'double reinforcement' can lead to impulsive/addictive behavior since every time we feel bored, anxious, angry, sad or lonely, we seek those things that both numb the bad feeling and distract our attention with pleasure.

How is Dopamine Fasting 2.0 based on Cognitive-Behavioral Therapy (CBT)?

We can regain flexibility over such automatic, rigid behavior by restricting the external stimuli, which is a Cognitive-Behavioral Therapy (CBT)-based technique called "stimulus control." You can do this in several ways to reduce your need to rely on willpower:

1) Put the stimulus (like your phone) away or make it harder to access.

2) Engage in an alternative activity that is incompatible with the stimulus (e.g. hard to do sports and stress eat at the same time)

3) Use website-blocking software or social accountability to prevent yourself from cheating.

We can also naturally expose ourselves to the internal stimuli (negative emotions), without engaging in the conditioned response (grabbing for our phone), which is another CBT-based technique called "exposure and response prevention".

1) Notice when the impulses arise, and what thoughts and feelings you're experiencing in that moment.

2) Practice "urge surfing": watch the desire to engage in the conditioned response come and go without giving into it.

3) Repeatedly returning to whatever you are doing on instead, with a spirit of non-judgement.

Over time, this weakens the classical conditioning in a process called 'habituation', which ultimately restores our behavioral flexibility.

Collectively, CBT is considered the gold standard treatment for impulse control disorders. With behaviors that are hard to abstain from altogether, the scientific consensus is that

"clinicians have generally agreed that moderated and controlled use of the Internet is most appropriate to treat the problem."

In addition, a specific study showed that dopamine fasting from Facebook for a week helped students regain 13.3 hours of their time, and significantly reduced depressive symptoms by 17%, which allowed them to engage in more healthy behaviors instead.

The Dopamine Fasting 2.0 Schedule:

What makes Dopamine Fasting 2.0 unique are the time blocks, which recommends fasting for gradually longer periods of time periodically to extend the benefits. Here's how to do it:

The FASTING Schedule (when you DON'T engage):

Follow the fasting schedule if you want to still do the behavior during the day, but just want to cut back a bit and regain some behavioral flexibility so it's not so impulsive all the time.

The fasting schedule excludes behaviors are problematic during periods of time that are normally associated with rest (nights/weekends/vacations), that make it easier to comply:

1–4 hours at the end of the day (depending on work & family demands)

1 weekend day (spent it outside on a Saturday or Sunday)

1 weekend per quarter (go on a local trip)

1 week per year (go on vacation!)

Remember these are suggested guidelines, not strict rules. If it's easier to start by dopamine fasting for 1 hour a day (vs. 4 hours a day), then go for it, and then try to ramp up to what you're willing to do and sustain long-term (e.g. 2 hours/day). Perfect is the enemy of good. So like Nike: just do it.

The FEASTING Schedule (when you DO engage):

If you would really like to minimize a behavior so you're doing it as little as is practically possible, but still want or need to do it on occasion, then add in the feasting schedule to put total time limitations about when exactly and how much you'll do the behavior.

With this added approach, allow yourself to engage in the behavior for 5–30 minutes, 1–3 times a day. One easy way of doing this, is allowing yourself to check your phone for notifications and communications right after mealtimes only for a limited amount of time before moving on.

Interestingly, the Chinese government has instituted a practice in-line with Dopamine Fasting 2.0 as compulsory law for minors under the age of 18. They use both and fasting and feasting schedules: having video game makers program a feature that disallows use from 10PM-8AM, and only allowing use for 1.5 hours/day during weekdays and 3 hours/day during weekends and holidays. While it would be ideal for parents to be the one to institute this, the Chinese are likely ahead of the curve here since they've seen how much internet addiction has devastated their youth.

What Makes Dopamine Fasting 2.0 Distinct?

Just as intermittent fasting has become all the rage in Silicon Valley, I have created "Dopamine Fasting 2.0" as the antidote to our overstimulated age. What differentiates Dopamine Fasting 2.0 is that I DO NOT prescribe a list of things that you cannot do. If you have zero bad habits that you would like to spend less time on, then you probably don't need to do it at all. However, if you find that a particular behavior is causing you:

- Distress (you're bothered by how much you do it)
- Impairment (interferes with your optimal social or school/work performance)
- Addictiveness (you want to cut down, but cannot consistently do so)

Then you may want to target that behavior for dopamine fasting. In my clinical experience, I find six categories of impulsive behaviors are commonly problematic and prone to addiction. Again, you DO NOT need to abstain from ALL of these things, only the ones that are an issue specifically for you. This also helps compliance, so you don't feel like you need to make drastic changes to your life and feel deprived:

- ❖ Emotional eating
- ❖ Internet/gaming
- ❖ Gambling/shopping
- ❖ Porn/Masturbation
- ❖ Thrill/novelty seeking
- ❖ Recreational drugs

This list is neither inclusive nor exclusive. The antiquated versions of "dopamine fasting" that say absolutely no digital devices, but I find this to be missing the point. For example, browsing compulsively through various articles on your phone can definitely be addictive, while reading a single book on a Kindle Paperwhite device (which has no options for distraction) is probably fine. To decide what to fast from, simply regard whether it's highly pleasurable or problematic for you, and thus you may need a break from.

The Six Most Common Behavioral Addictions:

1. Pleasure Eating

It's easier to be completely abstinent from recreational drugs, since they are not absolutely necessary to live or work. However, food is much trickier, since we obviously need to eat to sustain ourselves. Those those who are already doing intermittent fasting (IF; such as where you eat for 12 hours and fast for 12 hours) or extended fasting (where you fast for 1–5 days), it's very easy to incorporate into dopamine fasting. For example, the 4 hours of dopamine fasting + 8 hours of sleep = 12 hours of intermittent fasting that doesn't include food.

For everyone else, it's fine to eat healthy foods during a dopamine fast, just avoid those that tend to be highly rewarding/addictive. In my clinical experience, these are foods that are ultra-processed to have added ingredients that make them very:

Sweet (sugar-sweetened beverages)

Salty (chips)

Savory/Spicy (chili)

Combine carbs + fat (buttered popcorn, mac & cheese)

2. Internet/gaming

The internet is hard to avoid given how connected school/work is, so the goal is to compartmentalize it to within 12 hours, so your brain can take a break for the remaining 4 hours of the day and pursue valued activities instead.

Generally speaking, avoid anything designed by a company (movies/television) or involves frequent input (scrolling/clicking), since products such prioritize user engagement not user well-being. While the internet can be a great learning tool, the constant attentional switching (and thus dopaminergic firing) from social media, articles, forums, games, etc. is what's problematic. As mentioned, reading a book on a non-distracting digital device is fine.

3. Gambling/Shopping

These two behaviors are actually more related than people realize, given they involve repeatedly spending money in order to purchase a large payoff. They can be considered male and female cousins since more men like to gamble, and more women like to shop, though these stereotypes are increasingly blurring as traditional norms break down. In any case, any form of gambling and non-utilitarian shopping (for staples) should be avoided during a dopamine fast.

4. Porn/Masturbation

There's nothing intrinsically wrong with porn or masturbation on an individual level, but the issue is more around how they are used. For some people, these behaviors can become problematic and compulsive and thus benefit from dopamine fasting.

Sex is a trickier issue given there's another person involved, and thus may be hard to schedule. Thus, I'd suggest it's fine to have sex if you can't do it another time and it's done in a fulfilling way with a regular partner. Americans are generally starved of physical intimacy, so values-aligned sex is a healthy behavior worth making an exception for (just when I'm treating insomnia, I tell clients that sex is the only activity allowed in bed besides sleep, to promote sleep hygiene). Random Tinder hookups are obviously discouraged during a dopamine fast, as they can be impulsive/compulsive sexual behavior.

5. Thrill/novelty seeking

Psychologists call this "sensation seeking", the public calls it getting an "adrenaline rush". These behaviors can also take more subtle forms such as seeking novelty, complexity, & intensity (like watching a psychological thriller or horror movie).

An easy rule of thumb is if it elicits an emotion that is high energy/arousal AND very positive negative in quality/valence (such as euphoria or fear), then consider abstaining from it during a dopamine fast.

6. Recreational Drugs

Obviously abstain from recreational drugs during a dopamine fast, but that also includes alcohol and caffeine, which most people don't consider to be drugs because they're socially not stigmatized, but can absolutely be physiologically addictive. This also has the added health benefit of significantly improving your sleep quality if you avoid it in the 4 hours before your bedtime.

But I don't have time/can't avoid checking my phone!

If you can't fit your work/pleasure into 12–15 hours/day, I'd argue that you (who are not clinicians on call or first responders) are not very good at managing your time & energy. Learn to follow the 80/20 rule of figuring out what 20% of your behaviors are getting 80% of your results in order to figure out what to eliminate or delegate.

Forcing yourself to engage in "time-restricted pleasure" also makes you procrastinate less and better manage your time and energy, because you have to be efficient within that window.

What Should I Do Instead?

You don't need to "do nothing" or meditate during a dopamine fast (unless you'd like to). Just engage in regular activities that reflect your values:

- Health-Promoting (exercise, cooking)

- Leading (helping, serving others)

- Relating (talking, bonding over activities)

- Learning (reading, listening)

- Creating (writing, art)

What's Wrong With Fun? & "Dopamine Binges"

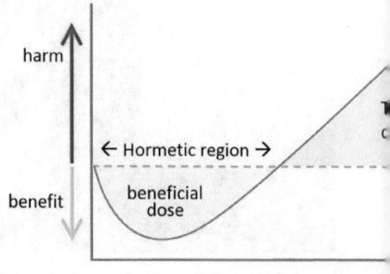

The point of dopamine fasting is not to encourage monasticism or masochism, Fun, enjoyment, and aesthetic appreciation are an important part of life (though most of could use less flattering social media and more fulfilling sex, which would honestly make us a lot happier).

Hormesis is a concept from toxicology where taking a substance in low doses may make us less susceptible/resilient to it over time. For example, being exposed to an allergen as a child may actually make you less allergic later in life. Similarly, I encourage going on "dopamine binges" once in a blue moon (obviously in a way that doesn't incur long-term health, relationships, or legal issues). That helps reinforce the lesson that these behaviors aren't inherently problematic, but it's the habit that's the issue. So practice flexibility regarding fasting itself in order to reset from resetting.

WHAT HAPPENS AFTER A FAST?

The buzz around dopamine fasting blew up around what people do (or don't do) during the fast itself. But in the long term, fasters must take additional steps if they aim to overcome their problematic behaviors.

"One of the things that happens when people initially cut themselves off from these rewards ... is that they suddenly become aware of themselves and their bodies in a new way," Lembke said. Without substances, screens or other stimuli to distract them, people suddenly become reacquainted with themselves, she said. "That, in fact, can be terrifying for people."

To move past these withdrawal periods and avoid relapse, people must address the roots of their addictive behaviors, Greenfield said. For example, people practicing compulsive internet use must learn how to place healthy limits on their use of the technology. Just like those addicted to drugs, they must come to recognize and cope with triggers that push them toward destructive behavior.

Mental health professionals can guide people through this process using standardized techniques like cognitive behavioral therapy (CBT), a protocol that helps people re-evaluate their patterns of thinking and behavior, and better cope with difficult situations, according to the American Psychological Association. (Sepah claims his recommended version of dopamine fasting is actually based on CBT techniques aimed at empowering people to overcome unhelpful impulses.)

"The idea is to ... temper our consumption" of rewards, Lembke said. In an age in which we enjoy easy access to addictive substances and a million other distractions pull at our attention, sometimes, we must "consciously abstain" from behaviors that could spiral out of control, she said.

That said, you probably shouldn't cut out all pleasurable experiences from your life, Greenfield added.

"I don't think it's realistic, and I'm not even sure it's healthy" to completely eliminate all pleasurable experiences, he said. "I am not familiar with any programs that advocate for that, and that's certainly not within the realm of typical medical treatment."

THE SCIENCE BEHIND A DOPAMINE FAST

There is a lot of evidence to suggest that a dopamine fast can have a positive impact in your life. Before we get too far though, let's address the elephant in the room. The brain is a complex thing and while dopamine is part of this, it's not the only factor that comes into play here. Dopamine is primarily in play with anticipatory pleasure and it could be argued other neurotransmitters play a larger role here. Calling this technique, a "dopamine detox" is a little bit of a misnomer, but not entirely inaccurate either, it's the phrase most people use, so let's run with it.

BASIC STEPS TO APPROACH DOPAMINE FASTING

Have you ever had a habit that you wish you could break, but just could not seem to find a way out of it? Sometimes bad habits can be a minor nuisance, but some behaviors can develop an addictive quality that prevents us from being productive and realizing our full potential. Taken to the extreme, these habits can negatively impact our ability to be social, ruin our professional ambitions, and keep us enslaved to meaningless life-wasting activities.

Essentially, the idea of dopamine fasting is to avoid activities that are producing excessive dopamine release as much as possible. Dr. Cameron Sepah writes that avoiding dopamine stimulating activities for extended periods of time will help you to reset your brain and let go of addictive behaviors.

The central subject topic of dopamine fasting is based in cognitive behavioral therapy (CBT). Dr. Sepah writes that the key to success is found in reducing excessive dopamine stimulating behaviors in small, regular, and manageable increments. You are essentially re-training your brain to be less influenced by emotion and desire by providing rational alternatives.

In other words, you don't have to go cold-turkey and live like a hermit monk. You still have a life and will be able to enjoy the things you like to do.

Identify the Stimulus – Whatever is Causing Addiction, Distress, or Impairment

Yes, I know that sounds obvious – but it may not be as straightforward as you might think. Some destructive behaviors are easy to recognize like eating too much, binging on pornography, or indulging in sugary drinks. Other dopamine stimulating behaviors can be much harder to pinpoint – like the unhealthy reliance on other people for your emotional validation (think social media).

Take a few days to be as self-aware as you can. Start a list of behaviors that you want to change, and give each behavior a rank. For example, you may find that you drink a little too much soda and you would like to cut down, but really it's not that bad (maybe you give it a 2), but that you spend way too much time on social media keeping tabs on comments (maybe you give that a 7).

Work on one behavior at a time. You can start on your lower ranked numbers first if you think that will be easier to get into the habit – or if you're feeling really determined, start with the worst of the worst.

Set a Fasting Schedule: set aside at least one day out of the week where you don't engage in the activity that you are working to reduce. If that seems too daunting, then perhaps you can set aside two half-days. The scheduling is completely up to you, but the idea is to develop a regularly scheduled pattern of avoidance to begin weaning yourself off of the behavior.

It's best to start small and ease into this – you don't want to become discouraged and quit before you give yourself the chance to succeed! Build up slowly by adding more time as you gain confidence.

Reward Yourself for Following Through

You did it! You got through your first scheduled week of dopamine fasting. As you progress, it's important to provide yourself with a new source of stimulation – but this time it will be from the accomplishment of sticking to your goals.

When choosing your reward, try to pick something that will not reinforce the behavior that you're trying to reduce. For example, having Coke as a reward for avoiding soda on your fast-day may be sending the wrong signal to yourself.

DOPAMINE FASTING: MISUNDERSTANDING SCIENCE SPAWNS A MALADAPTIVE FAD

The dopamine fast, created by California psychiatrist Dr. Cameron Sepah, has very little to do with either fasting or dopamine. As Sepah told the New York Times, "Dopamine is just a mechanism that explains how addictions can become reinforced, and makes for a catchy title. The title's not to be taken literally." Unfortunately, with such a snazzy name, who could resist? This is where the misconceptions begin.

What's the thinking behind a dopamine fast?

What Sepah intended with his dopamine fast was a method, based on cognitive behavioral therapy, by which we can become less dominated by the unhealthy stimuli — the texts, the notifications, the beeps, the rings — that accompany living in a modern, technology-centric society. Instead of automatically responding to these reward-inducing cues, which provide us with an immediate but short-lived charge, we ought to allow our brains to take breaks and reset from this potentially addictive bombardment. The idea is that by allowing ourselves to feel lonely or bored, or to find pleasures in doing simpler and more natural activities, we will regain control over our lives and be better able to address compulsive behaviors that may be interfering with our happiness.

The six compulsive behaviors he cites as behaviors that may respond to a dopamine fast are: emotional eating, excessive internet usage and gaming, gambling and shopping, porn and masturbation, thrill and novelty seeking, and recreational drugs. But he emphasizes that dopamine fasting can be used to help control any behaviors that are causing you distress or negatively affecting your life.

You can't "fast" from a naturally occurring brain chemical

Dopamine is one of the body's neurotransmitters, and is involved in our body's system for reward, motivation, learning, and pleasure. While dopamine does rise in response to rewards or pleasurable activities, it doesn't actually decrease when you avoid overstimulating activities, so a dopamine "fast" doesn't actually lower your dopamine levels.

Unfortunately, legions of people have misinterpreted the science, as well as the entire concept of a dopamine fast. People are viewing dopamine as if it was heroin or cocaine, and are fasting in the sense of giving themselves a "tolerance break" so that the pleasures of whatever they are depriving themselves of — food, sex, human contact — will be more intense or vivid when consumed again, believing that depleted dopamine stores will have replenished themselves. Sadly, it doesn't work that way at all.

Fasting may simply be a technique to reduce stress and engage in mindfulness-based practices

Sepah recommends that we start a fast in a way that is minimally disruptive to our lifestyles. For example, we could practice dopamine fasting from one to four hours at the end of the day (depending on work and family demands), for one weekend day (spend it outside on a Saturday or Sunday), one weekend per quarter (go on a local trip), and one week per year (go on vacation).

This all sounds sensible, if not necessarily new or groundbreaking. In fact, it sounds a lot like many mindfulness practices and good sleep hygiene, in the suggestion of no screen time before bed.

However, people are adopting ever more extreme, ascetic, and unhealthy versions of this fasting, based on misconceptions about how dopamine works in our brains. They are not eating, exercising, listening to music, socializing, talking more than necessary, and not allowing themselves to be photographed if there's a flash (not sure if this applies to selfies).

Misunderstanding science can create maladaptive behaviors

When you think that none of this is actually lowering dopamine, it's kind of funny! Especially since avoiding interacting with people, looking at people, and communicating with people was never part of Sepah's original idea. Human interaction (unless it is somehow compulsive and destructive) is in the category of healthy activities that are supposed to supplant the unhealthy ones, such as surfing social media for hours each day. In essence, the dopamine fasters are depriving themselves of healthy things, for no reason, based on faulty science and a misinterpretation of a catchy title.

Taking time out for mental rejuvenation is never a bad thing, but it's nothing new

The original intent behind the dopamine fast was to provide a rationale and suggestions for disconnecting from days of technology-driven frenzy and substituting more simple activities to help us reconnect us with ourselves and others. This idea is noble, healthy, and worthwhile, but it's certainly not a new concept. Most religions also suggest a rest day (for example, the Jewish Sabbath) or holidays without technological distractions, so that you can reflect and reconnect with family and community, Thousands of years of meditation also suggests that a mindful approach to living reaps many health benefits.

Unfortunately, the modern wellness industry has become so lucrative that people are creating snappy titles for age-old concepts. Perhaps that is how to best categorize this fad, if only we can get its proponents to look at us or speak to us, without disturbing their dopamine levels, in order to explain this to them.

WHAT TO KNOW ABOUT A DOPAMINE DETOX

A dopamine detox is a practice where you remove low quality stimuli from your life and replace it with high quality stimuli. This allows us to rid ourselves of cheap fixes in order to build a meaningful and fulfilling life. By doing this we take advantage of the dopaminergic responses in our brains along with a host of other neurotransmitters, to build long lasting, purposeful experiences. Modern life has been optimized to lean on these neurochemicals in a way, I'd argue, that is unhealthy, or at least justifies examination.

Dopamine detox is a concept which a lot of people follow. Consider it to be a detox, but for your brain. The simple rule to follow is to avoid engaging in any activity which you enjoy doing or which stimulates the brain-it could be browsing your phone, avoiding screentime, listening to music or engaging in any hobby. The idea is-to devoid the brain of any good happy activity, that, in the end, even a boring activity ends up being fun. That way, the brain starts to love it.

The idea of following such a detox plan sounds radical, but there's a smaller version of the plan which is easier to be followed. For one day each week, refrain from doing activities which seem pleasurable or dopamine boosting. This is a method to re-centre and refocus your brain on other activities which need attention. The detox plan is followed by a lot of high-thinkers and intellectuals, who credit this as a means of keeping sharp.

A dopamine detox entails fasting from dopamine producing activities, or "pleasures," for a certain amount of time with the hope of decreasing reward sensitivity. However, there is no scientific evidence to support this method.

Those who attempt a dopamine detox aim to detach themselves from everyday stimuli, such as social media, sugar, or shopping. They are replaced in favor of less impulsive habits and lifestyle choices. The fast can last for a few hours or several days.

It is very important to note that a dopamine detox is not a scientifically researched approach. Evidence of any benefits is anecdotal, and most benefits come from refraining from potentially addictive activities. However, they are not related to actually detoxing from dopamine.

The entire concept of a "dopamine detox" is scientifically incorrect, and reduces the brain to a very simplistic level. It is, in fact, far more complex that this "dopamine detox" trend suggests.

Dr. Cameron Sepah is the creator of the dopamine fast, or detox. He commonly uses the technique in clinical practice on tech workers and venture capitalists. Dr. Sepah's goal is to rid his clients of their dependence on certain stimuli, such as phone alerts, texts, and social media notifications. Much of his research around this new practice was based on cognitive behavioral therapy (CBT). What he was trying to accomplish with this concept is different from what people have come to understand that "dopamine detox" is.

The general concept behind Dr. Sepah's "detox" is for people to let themselves feel lonely or bored, or to try simpler activities instead of reaching for quick "hits" of dopamine. Ideally, people will start to notice how certain stimuli might distract them.

Dr. Sepah identifies six compulsive behaviors as targets of the dopamine detox as we have extensively talked about in preceding pages:

• emotional eating

• excessive internet usage and gaming

• gambling and shopping

• porn and masturbation

• thrill and novelty seeking

• recreational drugs

By fasting from these activities that trigger the brain's neurotransmitters, people become less dependent on the emotional "hits" that dopamine provides, which can sometimes lead to dependence or addiction.

DOES A DOPAMINE DETOX WORK?

Dopamine fasting stems from the idea that a constant barrage of junk food, porn, social media, recreational drugs, online shopping, and even professional success have dulled people's appreciation of the small pleasures in life. The hope is that intermittent bouts of asceticism will clear out the chemical receptors and reset dopamine levels in the brain, allowing people to experience and enjoy the small bursts in dopamine that come from everyday life instead of only responding to the large manufactured surges.

There's only one problem: That's not how dopamine works.

"This idea that dopamine is the buzz, the rush, the pleasure signal and all that... there's no evidence that [those feelings are] linked to dopamine at all!" says Jeff Dalley, a professor of psychology and psychiatry at the University of Cambridge who's studied the chemical for more than 20 years. Instead, he says, dopamine is "the stuff that happens beforehand, the appetitive motivation. The actual liking and all the hedonic effects we think is probably the opioid system."

During a dopamine detox, a person avoids dopamine triggers for a set period of time — anywhere from an hour to several days.

The dopamine detox requires a person to avoid any kind of arousal, specifically from pleasure triggers. Anything that stimulates dopamine production is off-limits throughout the detox.

Ideally, by the end of the detox, a person will feel more centered, balanced, and less affected by their usual dopamine triggers. However, it is important to note that a true dopamine detox, whereby a person successfully halts all dopamine activity in the brain, is not possible.

The human body naturally produces dopamine, even when it is not exposed to certain stimuli. A more accurate description of the dopamine detox is a period of abstinence, or "unplugging" from the world.

Doing so may have positive effects on those who implement the practice from time to time. However, the term "dopamine detox" by its very nature is problematic, and not at all scientifically correct. Dr. Sepah himself says the name is not meant to be interpreted literally.

THE DANGERS OF SOCIAL MEDIA, PHONES, AND MODERN LIFE

Several years ago, a sinking uneasiness sparked up about what social media, smart phones, the internet and modern life had become. It was a funny thing, because I've always been one who loves the internet and all things tech.

That's when a lot of studies started to come out about how suicide in teen girls jumped 300% because of social media and how phones and social media are leading to a rapid increase in depression and anxiety. The one thing that struck me the most was when Facebook's VP of User Growth stated "I have tremendous guilt. The short-term, dopamine-driven feedback loops that we have created are destroying how society works."

The dark foreboding feeling about various elements of modern life was not misattributed. Instead, I realized it was a very real factor of contention. After much searching and collecting my thoughts, I've been led to dopamine fasting as my response to the real challenges I face.

The question then becomes, how do we get rid of negative things in our lives that give us those hits of dopamine we're so easily drawn to? The truth is that it's really hard. The reason for this of course is because modern technology is perfectly optimized to abuse our dopamine system.

This is the root of low-level anxiety and depression in today's society and the very reason why these diagnoses are so prevalent. Over the past 20 years we've seen depression and anxiety rise dramatically and it's alarming. Simply put, we built a society that provides cheap and easy hits of dopamine as leverage for commercial profits and the bill for the true cost has come due.

Let's quickly think out of the box and look at the dominant tech lifestyle and consider Digital Minialism

WHAT IS DIGITAL DIGITAL MINIMALISM

Minimalism is big these days. In particular, there's a version of Minimalism called Digital Minimalism that's quickly rising to prominence as our lives become increasingly tech-centric.

Personal technology like smartphones and tablets are enabling us to spend more and more time online. And as we do, many of us are starting to feel uneasy about this persistent 'digital creep'—that steady march of gadgets and tech into every aspect of our lives.

We're starting to feel a little unsettled by how much time we spend staring at screens. And so, we're beginning to question the assumption that a steady stream of more and newer tech in our lives is an unqualifiedly good thing.

In response to this vague sense of tech dis-ease, a lot of us are looking for a way to think differently about tech and our relationship to it. And there's a sense that maybe this Minimalism thing is the place to start.

You're probably not surprised to hear that I do think Minimalism—and in particular, Digital Minimalism—is a great way to begin building a better, healthier relationship with our technology.

Digital Minimalism is a specific application of the general minimalist philosophy to the role of technology in our lives.

Cal Newport has the best definition of Digital Minimalism:

Digital minimalism is a philosophy that helps you question what digital communication tools (and behaviors surrounding these tools) add the most value to your life. It is motivated by the belief that intentionally and aggressively clearing away low-value digital noise, and optimizing your use of the tools that really matter, can significantly improve your life.

Just like physical stuff can be an impediment and distraction from what matters most in life, digital stuff can be as well. And as technology and the internet become an increasingly large part of our lives, their potential to distract us from what really matters grows larger every day.

The Digital Minimalist movement is a direct response to this threat. It's a call to action to take notice of and think carefully about our relationship with our technology; to be mindful and intentional about how much of our time and attention we really want to give to our technology, and what the tradeoffs of that decision are.

Basic Principles of Digital Minimalism

Digital Minimalism can mean a lot of things to a lot of people. To me, there are 3 essential principles that almost all of my thinking about Digital Minimalism flow from:

1. Technology use should be intentional, not habitual.

Because personal technology is increasingly powerful, available, and cheap, it's highly addictive. This addictive nature of personal technology means we're especially vulnerable to mindless and compulsive use, which is why it so easily interferes with our values and best intentions.

To guard against this mindlessness, we need to cultivate an intentional mindset for our tech use. This means that we use technology on purpose, not out of habit or routine. Being intentional with our tech makes it easier to be intentional with our values and the most important things in life.

2. Technology is for making stuff not feeling better.

One of the reasons it's so easy to misuse or overuse our technology is because it can be a powerful means of short-term emotional relief.

When we find ourselves bored, upset, tired, anxious, sad, angry, or just about any other uncomfortable feeling, it can be a relief to reach into our pockets and instantly lose ourselves to the comfortable numbness of cat videos on YouTube or interesting blog posts on Hacker News.

But short-term avoidance of emotional difficulty only leads to more consistent suffering in the long-term. The ability to so easily run away from our difficulties makes it that much more difficult to confront them when we must.

As an alternative to using tech for cheap emotional relief, we ought to use tech to make stuff—important, valuable, meaningful stuff.

As Cal Newport has said, "Humans, deep down, are craftsmen." We all have a desire on some level to create and produce.

From programming to poetry, we all have something to offer and give to the world, something to build.

Let's make that the primary goal for our technology.

Our lives have become tech-centric. It's starting to "own" us. It's time to seek ways to redesign our relationship with technology. Enter Digital Minimalism.

In 2007, Steve Jobs unveiled the future: the iPhone 3 and, along with it, the App Store. It marked the beginning of the mobile revolution, the era of the apps and streaming.

Not much later, Amazon introduced the Kindle. One of the oldest technology known to man became digital.

And, a year later, Google launched Chrome.

A little over a decade has passed but it seems like a century ago that our phones had a physical keyboard and we texted using SMS.

Ten years later we are addicted to technology. We crave for it. Here are alarming numbers from research:

Total digital media usage is up 40% since 2013

Smartphone usage has doubled in the last 3 years

1 of every 2 minutes spent online is on "leisure activities", such as social media, video viewing, entertainment/music, and games

1 of every 5 minutes spent online is on social media

The average person spends almost 3 hours per day on mobile

It's time to put an end to this madness. Life happens when you look up and around you, not screens.

How can we be more mindful around our technology?

Digital minimalism is the answer

Digital Minimalism: Using the Computer Intentionally

Let's start with the easiest one: setting up your computer to use it with intention.

The goal is to remove anything that is not adding value and double down on what we use on a regular basis.

Clean Up the Desktop: remove all the files and programs from your desktop. Use Spotlight to open them instead

Choose a Clean Wallpaper: it might seem trivial, but your wallpaper can have an impact on your productivity. Pick a photo that won't distract you but rather help you focus. I like Simple Desktops

Auto-Hide the Dock: you can set it up in the Dock preferences

Uninstall Programs: go through your apps and delete everything that you don't use

Install Updates: after clearing your unused apps, check for updates on the ones left and actually install them

Work in Full-Screen Mode: most programs offer full-screen mode, a perfect way to block out distractions

Digital Minimalism: Simplifying Files

Time to graduate to something a little more tricky: files.

As hard drives get bigger we tend to accumulate a lot of digital junk on our computers. Over time, it's harder to find what we need.

It's time to stop that. Here's how:

Delete: first up is deleting all the files you don't need

Upload to the Cloud: now split your files into two categories: the ones you use regularly and the ones you don't. For the later, upload them to the cloud. The major contenders are photos and old files you don't need

Make Content Searchable: choose easy to remember names for your folders and files so you can always find anything quickly using search

Fewer Folders: search is so powerful now that filling becomes a thing of the past. Use fewer but bigger folders. I have "Work", "Personal", and "Fun" and then just search inside each one of them for what I need

Clear to Neutral: at the end of the day, close all your tabs and programs, delete or move all the files from Downloads, empty the trash, and shut off your computer. By clearing to neutral you're helping "future you" get started

Access, Don't Own: ownership can be stressful. Instead, take advantage of the access economy by streaming video and music

Digital Minimalism: A Better Phone Experience

Next up, let's tackle something a little bigger: our phone.

A little over a decade these devices didn't exist. So how come they are such a big part of our lives now?

Here's the step-by-step for digital minimalism on your phone and all-around a better experience:

Remove Apps: as with the computer, start by deleting all the apps you don't use anymore. For apps you use but not frequently consider using the browser version

A Mindful Home Screen: place the 4 most used apps on your dock at the bottom. Put everything else into a single folder

Clean Up Contacts: browse through your contact list and delete numbers you won't need ever again

Delete: the prime candidates are podcasts and music you don't listen to anymore. Stream instead of downloading

Now Use Search: you can use spotlight not only to find apps but also content within them, like finding someone's phone number by typing their name. Search is your new best friend

Remove Notifications: leave phone calls and text messages but remove all the other notifications. Trust me, the world won't come to an end. When you want to check something, open the app and do so. Don't let the app control you to open it

Do Not Disturb: schedule Do Not Disturb after working hours so you can relax, such as from 8 PM to 8 AM

Digital Minimalism: Escaping Email Hell

The average adult checks their email 45 times.

Yet nobody has claimed to have changed the world by checking email.

Treat email as a to-do and schedule it in your calendar. Only check email twice per day: late morning and late evening.

Technology should never come before people.

Despite the perpetual promise of the internet and social media to make us more connected, personal technology is all too often a source of isolation and disconnect from other people in our lives.

How many tiny, glorious moments of my daughter's life have I missed because I was checking how well a recent tweet did?

How many fascinating conversations and relationships have I missed out on because I instantly pop in headphones and put on a podcast the minute I sit down in my seat on a plane or bus?

How many family gatherings are ruined by ridiculous Facebook posts?

This constant reminder to put people before tech is arguably the most important aspect of Digital Minimalism.

Living better with less technology

Our lives used to be simple. With the advancement of technology, there are changes that we have made to our lifestyle. High technology (also referred now to as "smart tech"), whose goal is to make our lives easy, turned out to be one of the biggest problems of the modern digital world. We always have this urge to buy the latest and the greatest gadgets and appliances. Sometimes to impress people that we don't even know on social media, or tolerate our lazy reliance on the new technology. Is going "smart" really a smart decision?

What is a Low Tech Lifestyle?

While techy people always want the newest and the greatest, people living in low tech lifestyle always want to get the most out of their existing technologies. They are not the people who entirely deprive themselves of the latest technology. Instead, they are people who still work on 5-year-old laptop or computers which still "gets the job done".

What's the sense of wasting money if your old one still works, right? If the old technology you have right now is still economical to use and gives you a performance enough to finish the job, there's no sense of upgrading to the smarter ones.

Low tech lifestyle is not only about not "excessively" buying the latest gadgets and appliances, but it also refers to a lifestyle we have pre-social media. The era of sanity.

People living with this lifestyle try not to rely much on social media, or altogether remove social media out of their lives. Facebook and Instagram, for example, has been a part of our daily routine. We sleep and wake up with our phones, reading other people's problems or success on these platforms.

Imagine having a rough time, and seeing our Facebook friend's success and our favourite influencer's new travel getaway. Sometimes, it makes us question ourselves why we don't have the same level of success as them, despite working 8-12 hours a day.

We Don't Talk Anymore

Newer technology also distracts us from reality. Ten years ago, when we go out with our friends, we always had long conversations. Today, when we go out with our friends, 8 out of 10, it's just all about eating and scrolling on our phone at a restaurant. Sure, a short "how are you", or "how's life been…", while staring at our phone's display but that's as far as conversations go.

Some restaurants (like the Hearth restaurant in Manhattan) now collect people's phone to help customers not get distracted from enjoying their meals and real-world conversations. Tech companies such as Google also join the movement with it's a mandatory implementation of "Digital Wellbeing" feature on all Android devices running Android 8 and above. Digital Wellbeing tracks where you spend most of your time when using your smartphone.

Sometimes, social media cost us our peace of mind that some of us resort to "tech detox". Tech detox is a mind rehab which aims to refrain us from relying much on high technology, clearly from our gadgets and social media for a specific period. While tech detox is just a temporary activity, low living tech is for a lifetime for many. Not only does it save time and money, but most of all, our sanity.

How to Live a Low Tech Lifestyle?

Living a low tech lifestyle is not that hard to start with. What you have now (including your phone, TV, and laptop) is what you're living with for the few years.

As I've said, the goal here to get the most out of our existing technologies. If you're still using a CRT television, you are free to replace it because it is no longer economical. But if you're using a 4K UHD television, is upgrading to another 4K UHD television necessary? Also, if you still have an LCD TV with HDMI, you can take advantage of some mediacasters like Roku, Amazon Fire TV stick, or Chromecast to make it smart! No need to shell out an extra $400 or more to spend on a smart TV. With the right Mediacaster, any TV can be smart.

An android phone usually gets an update for up to 3 years. Two years for major OS upgrade, and 3 years for security patches (based on Android One). I have friends who always work their asses out to buy the newest model of their favourite brand, just less than a year after the release of the previous model.

Android users are the most vulnerable when it comes to switching phones. Android phones are much cheaper and more diverse than the iPhone, so users think their Android phone is disposable and take for granted all the things a cheap phone can offer. However, you can always use different themes or launchers to change the User Experience of your phone. Even you can switch your normal text messenger to some customized messenger or you can download GBWhatsapp instead of a normal WhatsApp which will give you more options for customization.

As I've said, low living tech is not just all about gadget and appliances. It also means living your life surrounded by "real" surroundings. Removing social media in your life is not easy. I have a hard time doing this too. Here's the thing, I created another account for this specific purpose and deactivated my personal account. I didn't add anyone who is not essential to me.

Doing this will reduce the number of notifications you receive daily and will, therefore, save you a lot of time. You can do the same for Twitter, Instagram and Snapchat as well.

If you want to rant to something, do it. We usually want to let the world know what we feel. After a few people have seen and reacted to it, set your audience to "Only Me". So, what's the sense of ranting then? Well, letting someone see it, gives you a certain satisfaction. And if you get this satisfaction, it's time to make it private, so you don't get more notifications.

But have you realized one thing? This used to be the job of a diary. A diary helps us let our feelings out, without having to worry about how people react to it. It never wastes our time, because you have no notifications to reply to.

Benefits of Living a Low Tech Lifestyle

Living a low tech lifestyle is all about enjoying real-world life, saving money, time, and restoring the classic lifestyle we have pre-social media days. As I've said, there's no need to buy a new phone or computer if it still gets the job done. Don't waste money on something that you have! Get the most out of your existing technologies before finally deciding for an upgrade. Getting smart gadgets and appliances is not as good as trusting yourself and your senses. Yes, there are things we can't do, but come to think of it. We never really think we needed one until it suddenly just exists in the market.

Social media has become a waste of time, and living in a real-world is way better than living on social media! Yes, life is stressful but let me tell you this, social media is hundred times more stressful! Imagine getting bashed after saying an opinion. Using Social media is letting yourself get involved too much on things that make you depressed. Of all things. Not healthy. Instead of posting on social media, try writing a diary.

One more thing, living low tech makes us appreciate even intangible things such as darkness and silence. Here's a snippet from David Maddalena's book title "(low) tech writer":

"I love it when the power goes out. I'm not immune to the inconvenience: I am a computer user after all (note that I don't publish these essays on parchment paper). But if the power does go out, I will save my work, fold my laptop up, and revel in the silence and the dark. To light candles and be in the beautiful glow of little flames and listen to the subtle, natural sounds. It's a little unplanned vacation from modernity. I am glad for the conveniences of electricity. But there are always consequences that result from our tireless pursuit of convenience."

WHY WE NEED TO RE-ENGAGE WITH THE REAL WORLD

Many of us spend hours every day tethered to our devices, pawing at the screen to see if it will deliver a few more likes or emails, monitoring the world and honing our online presence. Social networking platforms such as Whatsapp, Snapchat, Instagram, Facebook and Twitter are supposed to make us feel more connected. Yet our reliance on technology to "see" the social world around us can be a heavy burden that we are disconnected from the real word.

To Quit Social Media …

Quitting social media is not just a trend or something to make you seem ultra-enlightened. Research has revealed some valid reasons why you might want to toss aside your virtual networks.

Happiness and Mood

Our happiness is one of the most important aspects of our lives. Still, we check on the very thing that might be chipping away at our happiness dozens – or hundreds! – of times a day.. Studies have shown that social media can have a negative effect on your life satisfaction and subjective well-being. Evidence also suggests that social media is linked to depressive symptoms.

We know more about the end result, that those who use social media more tend to be less satisfied, than we do about what causes this result. Social comparison is often cited, because your friends are likely posting about the new job they got and not the 14 jobs they applied for and didn't get before that. Looking at others' perpetual highlight reel, versus your own behind-the-scenes life, can make you feel inadequate if you don't feel like you have anything "post-worthy" at the moment. The Happiness Research Institute also found that people on Facebook had trouble concentrating, felt less present and thought they were wasting their time at a higher rate than peers not using Facebook.

If you're on social media a lot, enough research suggests that you might want to run your own little experiment to see if a social media break or decrease can boost your mood.

Self-Esteem

What if you can't hit those selfie angles quite like a Kardashian? (P.s. They hired a photographer for that "selfie.") Or your entire Facebook community seems to be getting promotions while you can't seem to impress your boss or get ahead at work?

Social media makes you a lot more aware of what is happening in your world and if you feel like you don't stack up to those around you it can have a negative effect on your self-esteem. The era of filters, Instagram models and influencers, online fitness celebrities and readily available photo-editing tools can be particularly burdensome on our self-esteem. Two studies looked particularly at the effect of selfies and determined that looking at others' selfies harmed self-esteem and caused women to compare themselves negatively to others. Another study found that social media use correlated with feeling unattractive.

Going back to social comparisons, Facebook might also be making you feel less successful in your career and relationships.

In just minutes, you can easily be inundated with images of people who seemingly have it better than you in one way or another. Just remember that social media is not real life and every post is made by a person (Well, except for the bots. Actually, there are a lot of bots posting.) and that person has ups and downs, too.

Sleep

So many of us are not getting enough sleep. In fact, the Centers for Disease Control and Prevention (CDC) reported that 35 percent of Americans don't get the recommended seven hours of sleep a night. But when it comes time to actually go to sleep so many of us get in our comfortable pajamas and cuddle up cozilly with a ...

cold chunk of glass, metal and plastic that emits a hue of light and messages that inhibit our sleep.

Yes, the light from our devices, particularly the blue hue that is common, is disruptive to sleep in itself. And one study found that young adults who check social media more frequently and for more time, have greater sleep disturbances.

And given the impact sleep has on the rest of our health, it's wise to find a way to detach your phone from your bedtime routine.

7-day plan to digital minimalism

It's almost like counters that clutter with random things, knick-knacks, and recycling. Unless you have a system for where things go, they'll continue to pile up. Then when you need something you have no idea where it is. In addition to that, with digital clutter, there is the constant issue of notifications that scream for attention.

In his insightful TEDx video Chris Bailey says that on average we focus on anything for just 40 seconds before we are interrupted. I have Slack, Whatsapp and Instagram constantly pinging and despite telling myself not to, I always stop what I'm doing to check. It was the video and seeing how little I was getting done that prompted me to do a seven-day Digital Minimalism experiment.

The plan wasn't a complete detox, it was just to set up some guidelines that I planned to follow through for seven days. I knew it was going to be a challenge, which is why I limited myself to 4 simple rules.

The Rules

No screens in bed

According to the NHS, sleep hygiene comprises of several factors. One of them is to avoid using smartphones, tablets, or other electronic devices for an hour or so before you go to bed. It's not rocket science, we all know that phones and screens overstimulate our brains. I knew that this rule would be the most challenging for me. I usually spend the first and last 30 minutes of each day mindlessly scrolling through social media.

2. Schedule email to twice daily

I tend to have my inbox open on a tab all the time when I'm working. I wasn't getting emails every second but I'd keep absently checking. I decided that 30 minutes in the morning and 30 minutes before I shut down my laptop would be enough to stay on top of emails and not miss replying to anything.

3. Limit social media

A huge chunk of my time on social media is spent on mindlessly consuming content. I watch everything from cute animal videos to cooking videos, DIY projects to fashion. I don't have any pets, I am not an expert chef, I don't want to build furniture, and I have no idea about fashion. There was no need for me to be watching all these videos. I decided to leave my phone in the kitchen to avoid the temptation to reach for it.

4. Limit all streaming to one day

It could be YouTube, Netflix, Amazon Prime, or Vimeo but I allowed myself to only stream content on Friday. I figured it would be a good segue into the weekend and would be a reward for a whole workweek of Digital Minimalism.

Does this seem crazy to you? Once I drew up my plan it seemed insane to me. I was a little worried that I might miss out on an important assignment, or that my social relationships would suffer. However, I figured seven days is not a huge commitment and this was at least worth a try.

The beginning (Day 1 and 2)

I checked my emails in the morning and settled into work. All-day, I kept thinking about my inbox and was anxious. I was also constantly reaching for my phone and had to remind myself that my phone was sitting in the kitchen. I enjoyed making lunch, it was relaxing somehow. As the day wore on and I came closer to my email/ social media time I got excited.

The middle (day 3,4 and 5)

I still had the same anxiety and excitement as the previous two days, just milder this time. I had a weak moment where I typed gmail.com into my browser without even thinking and then couldn't help checking. Instead of satisfying me, it made me guilty and I was surprised about this development. Day 5 was exciting because I allowed myself to watch a couple of episodes of The Office. I didn't want to start a new show and get addicted. I was surprised at how easy it was to stop watching. In the past, I've binge-watched entire seasons in one go at times.

The end (day 6, 7)

By now I was well adjusted, again I was surprised at how easily this happened. Because I had fixed times with limits for email and social media I found that I was focussed on being more efficient with both and cutting through the noise.

The entire experiment turned out to be much easier than I imagined it would. The single greatest takeaway for me was scheduling social media. It's so easy to lose myself in the rabbit hole of Instagram and neglect work that I know I should be doing. This experiment showed me that I wasn't missing anything, and could still enjoy my favorite apps if I was disciplined about it. Despite the strict limits I placed I didn't miss any important emails, or social commitments either.

If you're on the fence about this whole thing and you're not sure if Digital Minimalism is for you I recommend reading Digital Minimalism by Cal Newport. It might make you question a lot of assumptions you have about your use of technology, especially social media.

Digital declutter best practices/ways to reduce digital clutter

Whether you're juggling lots of creative projects or seeking inspiration for the next big one, taking the time to clear your digital clutter can make all the difference in your workflow. Research shows that digital disorganization can be just as anxiety-inducing as a messy physical space. The stress doesn't really go away when we turn off our screens, and we know it. Often, the only way to regain peace of mind is to roll up your sleeves and get rid of the digital clutter once and for all.

Just the simple act of organizing your digital clutter can help reduce stress and leave you feeling calm and recharged. If you're feeling overwhelmed, we've got five simple tips to get ahead of the chaos and achieve a state of intentional, well-organized bliss. Just like Marie Kondo's KonMari Method, we're going to give you five simple categories to approach organizing your digital clutter once and for all. You don't need to be a digital hoarder to benefit from these practices. Trust us — even if you can already find everything you need, this is going to be like a spa day for your workflow. So, light a scented candle, take a deep breath, and let's dive in.

- ➢ Deal with Your Desktop Files
- ➢ Purge Your Inbox
- ➢ Clean Up Your Font Collection

- ➢ Organize Your Digital Assets
- ➢ Break Bad Browser Habits
- ➢ Deal with Your Desktop Files

If the first thing you see when you turn on your computer is a desktop full of digital clutter, you're not off to a peaceful start for your day. A busy desktop isn't just an eyesore. It can actually slow down your computer. And if you've ever had to screen share and show your messy desktop to your coworkers, it can be just as embarrassing as a messy work station or personal space.

The amount of digital clutter on your desktop can actually say a lot about your personality and approach to workflow. It doesn't necessarily indicate being "disorganized" at all. But even if you can find absolutely everything you need in that sea of files, creating a system for storing and organizing digital assets on your computer can help you feel more organized and calmer throughout your workday. It creates a foundation for organized digital asset management, and it's also one of the fastest digital declutter projects on this list.

When it comes getting your desktop digitally organized, don't let perfection be the enemy of progress. This task can usually be accomplished pretty quickly. Just fifteen or twenty minutes is usually plenty of time to get even the most chaotic of desktops in order. Carve out some dedicated time on your calendar, put on a favorite playlist, and watch how quickly you can get rid of digital clutter on your desktop.

Start by creating a few basic folders to categorize all the photo assets, design files, and documents on your desktop. Drag and drop your digital assets into those folders. Add additional folders as needed and consider the nested folder structure to make things even tidier. Our article about creating a manageable folder structure is intended for company-wide organization, but it has some great tips for creating a digital asset management folder structure — even if it's just for your own personal use.

Whenever this is done, it is discovered that there are a lot of duplicates of photo assets, early versions of creative work, and other stuff that just isn't relevant anymore. Organizing the digital clutter on your desktop can also be a great opportunity to delete digital assets that are no longer useful. As a finishing touch, select "Clean Up" on Mac or try adding fences on a Windows desktop. Now, your desktop isn't just clean, it's straightened up.

2. Get Rid of Digital Clutter in Your Inbox

Fun fact: it never occurred to me to delete my emails until my mid-20s. And can you blame me? There's information in there! Why would I ever get rid of it?

It's true that hoarding emails ensure you always have certain information, but it can actually make it harder to search and find the exact email you need. If you're looking for a specific important email, and your search is turning up dozens of emails, it may be time to clear your digital clutter and purge your inbox. Like a cluttered desktop, a jam-packed inbox can also slow things down.

You don't need to aspire to an empty inbox. The goal here is simply to get rid of digital clutter: older, irrelevant, and useless emails.

Here are a few tips for cleaning out your inbox:

This process is usually faster and easier on a computer than on a mobile device.

You can begin with older emails, where you're more likely to find outdated information.

For emails with attachments, save necessary attachments to well-organized local folders, then delete the emails if they have no other purpose.

For emails with work information, ask yourself if that information is available somewhere else — a project management space, a single source of truth, etc. If the information is accessible elsewhere and you can find it easily, you probably don't need to hold on to the email.

Creating and maintaining an inbox free of digital clutter takes time and routine maintenance. Depending on how many emails you have, this might be more of an ongoing process than a one-time task, or you could follow Fast Company's guide to cleaning up your inbox in one hour if you're ready for a digital declutter sprint. You're also bound to become even more comfortable deleting unnecessary emails as you receive and read them, which will help you stay digitally organized going forward.

3. Clean Up Your Font Collection

It's not uncommon for designers to have hundreds or even thousands of fonts. We get it. Fonts are awesome. But absolutely no one, not even the greatest typography geek among us, can memorize that many fonts.

If you use fonts on a regular basis and haven't already invested in a font management solution, we'd recommend getting an amazing font manager to save time and make your life easier. The right font manager can handle more fonts than any human brain ever could, all while integrating with your creative tools, improving consistency, and speeding up your workflow.

If you're using any of Extensis' font management solutions, you also have the ability to organize your font collection how you want. Many designers choose to organize by style (such as sans-serif vs. serif), project, or client. Others choose to organize their collections by font foundry or type designer. Since we all take different approaches to organization, it's important to clean up your font collection in a way that feels intuitive and sustainable for your workflow.

If you absolutely love your fonts, taking the time to organize them can be a truly enjoyable way to clear your digital clutter.

4. Organize Your Digital Assets

As you work on getting your own workflow and asset collections more organized, it's also worth considering the digital assets that you and your team use together. Just like our own inboxes and desktops can become full of digital clutter, repositories for brand assets are also susceptible to disorganization.

If your team has an established system for storing and sharing digital assets in place, workflow can usually stay well organized, but routine maintenance is always helpful. It can also be useful to rethink your digital asset management folder structure if your needs have changed over time, as you've acquired significantly more assets.

Before you decide to start organizing digital assets for your team, get the all-clear from management, and check in with them before making any major decisions that could alter workflow. It's also common courtesy to alert your team to significant changes.

Here are some of the most effective ways to tidy up your DAM:

If recent and current projects aren't organized, expand your folder structure as needed and assign the projects' assets to where they belong.

Ask coworkers and teammates to add all relevant files from individual devices to ensure all assets can be managed.

Consider archiving assets that are no longer needed, so that they don't show up in search results.

Organizing digital assets for your team's workflow won't just make your life easier, it will also be appreciated by your colleagues. You can learn more about digital asset management here.

5. Break Bad Browser Habits

Multiple tabs can be a matter of love and hate. Some people find multiple tabs to be the epitome of digital clutter. Personally, I love opening multiple tabs in a browser window and using them like items on a to-do list. I work from left to right, closing out tabs as I complete the tasks associated with them. As a content writer, I do a ton of online research. Where some people might see digital clutter in my tabs, I see an effective workflow for skimming information and completing tasks.

The only problem is that tabs inevitably pile up, leading to incredibly crowded windows. It's easy for our browsers to go from functionally organized to a full-fledged digital hoarding within a matter of hours. The tabs go from being helpful to being an impediment. And, you guessed it, too many tabs can also slow down your computer.

From a self-identified tab fiend, here's what I find helpful when you want to clear your digital clutter and get back down to one tab:

Start using your browser's bookmark function more diligently. This is a great way to stash resources for later without keeping them in separate tabs. Organizing separate bookmark folders makes this even more effective.

Delete tabs as soon as you're "done" with them if applicable. This means that once that post-meeting Zoom tab pops up, delete it. Once you've read an article and gotten when you need from it, close it.

If you're really in a bind, take a shortcut and sweep it under the rug. Plugins like OneTab allow you collapse all your tabs into one for when you need a fresh start, or if you just want to screen share without shame.

There you have it: five approaches to organizing digital clutter once and for all. May your workdays be free of clutter and chaos.

Device usage and anxiety

The Link between Cell Phone Use, Anxiety, and Depression Nearly 5 billion people use mobile phones throughout the world, while 3 billion users access the Internet on a regular basis. Unfortunately, a new study suggests this activity could indicate anxiety and depression, especially when people use technology to escape from stress.

A Security Blanket

In a two-part study aimed at assessing how cell phone use might impact mental health, researchers at the University of Illinois surveyed 300 undergraduate students. After reviewing the answers to several strategic questions, the researchers found that subjects who described themselves as having addictive-style behaviors toward cellphones and the Internet scored much higher on anxiety and depression scales.

In the second part of the study, these same researchers asked 72 undergraduates to spend five minutes writing about a weakness or personal flaw that made them feel uncomfortable. They then left the subjects alone for several minutes while they "reviewed" the answers. During this time, one-third of the participants were allowed access to their cellphones, while another third enjoyed access to computer games and the final third enjoyed no access to any sort of technology.

After a follow-up assessment, researchers found that subjects who were allowed to use their cellphones were 64 percent less likely to experience anxiety. At the same time, they found that 82 percent of the anxious members of the cellphone group turned to their devices during the waiting time, while only half of non-anxious members chose to access their phones.

The Chicken or the Egg?

Appearing in the publication, Computers in Human Behavior, this recent study seems to indicate a strong tie between depression, anxiety and cell phone use. That said, it's not clear whether technology has a causal effect or if it merely provides an escape for people experiencing negative feelings.

According to the researchers, their study does not suggest that smartphones cause negative psychological conditions. After all, it is absolutely reasonable to assume that people will look for distractions during times of emotional stress. Still, addictive cell phone behaviors could be a strong indicator of depression or anxiety. Armed with this knowledge, parents may have an easier time noticing when their children are struggling with emotional or psychological issues.

Digital detox

What Is a Digital Detox?

A digital detox refers to a period of time when a person refrains from using tech devices such as smartphones, televisions, computers, tablets, and social media sites. "Detoxing" from digital devices is often seen as a way to focus on real-life social interactions without distractions. By forgoing digital devices, at least temporarily, people can let go of the stress that stems from constant connectivity.

Before you decide if it is right for you, consider some of the potential benefits and methods of doing a digital detox.

Reasons for a Digital Detox

For many people, being connected and immersed in the digital world is just a part of everyday life. According to research from the Nielsen Company, the average U.S.

adult spends around 11 hours each day listening to, watching, reading, or interacting with media.

There are many reasons why you might want to give up your mobile phone and other devices for a brief time. You might want to enjoy time to yourself without the interference that your phone and other devices create. In other cases, you might feel like your device use has become excessive and is adding too much stress to your life.

In some situations, you might even feel like you are addicted to your devices. While technology addiction is not formally recognized as a disorder in the DSM-5, many experts believe that tech and device overuse represents a very real behavioral addiction that can lead to physical, psychological, and social problems.

In a poll conducted by the organization Common Sense Media, 50% of teens reported that they felt that they were addicted to their mobile devices. A whopping 78% of the teen respondents said that they check their digital devices hourly.

What the Research Says

Technology Can be Stressful

While people often feel that they can't imagine life without their tech devices, research and surveys have found that technology use can also contribute to stress.

In the American Psychological Associations' annual Stress in America survey, a fifth of U.S. adults (around 18%) cited technology use as a significant source of stress in their life. For many, it is the ever-present digital connection and constant need to keep checking emails, texts, and social media that accounted for the majority of this tech stress.

One study conducted by researchers in Sweden found that heavy technology use among young adults was linked to sleeping problems, depressive symptoms, and increased stress levels.

Digital Devices Can Disrupt Sleep

Evidence also suggests that heavy device use, particularly prior to bedtime, can interfere with sleep quality and quantity. One study found that children who use digital devices at bedtime had significantly worse and less sleep. The study also found a connection between nighttime tech use and increased body mass index.

Researchers have also found that in-bed electronic social media use has adverse effects on sleep and mood. The study found that 70% of participants checked social media on their phones while in bed, with 15% spending an hour or more on social media while in bed. The results found that using social media when you are in bed at night increases the likelihood of anxiety, insomnia, and shorter sleep duration.

How Your Smartphone Affects Your Brain

Heavy Device Use May Be Linked to Mental Health Concerns

A study published in the journal Child Development found that heavy daily technology use was associated with an increased risk for mental health problems among adolescents. More time spent using digital technologies was linked to increased symptoms of ADHD and conduct disorder, as well as worse self-regulation.

Researchers from the University of Pennsylvania recently published the first experimental research linking the use of social media sites such as Facebook, Snapchat, and Instagram to decreased well-being. The results revealed that limiting social media use decreased symptoms of depression and loneliness.

Constant Connectivity Affects Work/Life Balance

That feeling of always being connected can make it difficult to create boundaries between your home life and work life. Even when you are at home or on vacation, it can be hard to resist the temptation to check your email, respond to a text from a colleague, or check in on your social media accounts.

In a study published in the journal Applied Research in Quality of Life, researchers found that technology use played a role in determining an individual's work-life balance. The study suggested that the use of internet and mobile technologies influenced overall job satisfaction, job stress, and feelings of overwork.

Doing a digital detox may help you establish a healthier, less stressful work-life balance.

Social Comparison Makes It Hard to Be Content

If you spend time on social media, you have probably found yourself comparing your own life to your friends, family, total strangers, and celebs. You might find yourself thinking that everyone else seems to be leading a fuller, richer, or more exciting life based on the tiny, curated glimpse you see on their Instagram or Facebook posts.

As the saying goes, comparison really can be the thief of joy. Detoxing from your social connections can be a good way to focus on what's important in your own life without comparing yourself to others.

 The Stress of Social Comparison

Digital Connectivity Can Make You Feel Like You're Missing Out

Fear of missing out, known as FOMO, is the fear that you are missing the experiences that everyone else is having. Constant connectivity can feed this fear. Every time you see a curated image or post about someone else's life, it can leave you feeling as if your life is less exciting than theirs. You might find yourself overcommitting to social events out of the fear that you'll be left behind.

FOMO can also keep you constantly checking your device out of fear that you are going to miss an important text, DM, or post.

Doing a digital detox is one way to set limits and reduce your fear of missing out. The key is to do it in a way that doesn't leave you feeling cut off from what's happening in your digital world.

Signs You Might Need a Digital Detox

You feel anxious or stressed out if you can't find your phone

You feel compelled to check your phone every few minutes

You feel depressed, anxious, or angry after spending time on social media

You are preoccupied with the like, comment, or reshare counts on your social posts

You're afraid that you'll miss something if you don't keep checking your device

You often find yourself staying up late or getting up early to play on your phone

You have trouble concentrating on one thing without having to check your phone

Are You Addicted to Your Phone?

How to Do a Digital Detox

Some might suggest that a true digital detox would involve predefined abstinence from any and all digital devices and social media connections, but it is important to make your device usage work for your own life and demands.

Detaching from your devices can benefit your mental well-being, but doing a digital detox does not have to involve a complete separation from your phone and other tech connections. The process is often more about setting boundaries and making sure that you are using your devices in a way that benefit, rather than harm, your emotional and physical health.

Be Realistic

If you can do a complete digital detox for a certain amount of time, it might be something you want to try. Being completely disconnected can feel liberating and refreshing for some people. For a lot of people, completely forgoing all forms of digital communication might not be possible, particularly if you really do rely on staying connected for work, school, or other obligations.

This doesn't mean that you can't enjoy the benefits of a digital detox; the key is to make disconnecting something that works for your schedule and your life.

If you need your devices during the day for your job, try doing a mini-detox at the end of the workday. Pick a time when you want to turn off your devices, and then focus on spending an evening completely free of things like social media, texting, online videos, and other electronic distractions.

Set Limits

While it isn't always possible or even preferable to completely disconnect, setting limits on when these digital connections are allowed to intrude on your time can be good for your mental well-being.

For example, you might want to use your phone to play your Spotify or Apple Music playlist while you are working out, but setting it to airplane mode will make sure that you aren't distracted by phone calls, texts, other messages, or app notifications during your workout.

Setting boundaries on the type and timing of connections you'll attend to helps ensure that you can enjoy real-world activities completely free of digital diversions.

Other times when you might want to limit your digital device usage include:

When you are eating meals, particularly when dining with other people

When you are waking up or going to bed

When you are working on a project or hobby

When you are spending time with friends or family

Before you go to sleep each night

Research suggests that limiting your social media use to approximately 30 minutes per day can significantly improve well-being, decreasing symptoms of loneliness and depression.7

Restricting your mobile device usage immediately before you go to sleep may also be helpful. One review of the research found that using media devices was linked to poor sleep quality, inadequate sleep, and excessive daytime sleepiness. Skip laying in bed playing on your phone and instead try reading a book or magazine for a few minutes before you go to sleep.

Remove Distractions

Another way to start your digital detox is to turn off push notifications on your phone. Many social media apps including Facebook, Instagram, Twitter, Pinterest, and news websites send alerts every single time you get a message, mention, or new post.

Rather than checking certain apps or websites every time a new story or post hits, set aside a specific time each day when you'll check your messages or mentions. Then set aside a certain amount of time, around 20 or 30 minutes, to devote to catching up and sending responses.

You might find that it's helpful to leave your phone behind for at least a brief time. Studies have found that the mere presence of a mobile device, even if you aren't actively using it, lowers empathy levels and decreased conversation quality when interacting with other people, a phenomenon researchers have dubbed 'the iPhone effect.'10

So the next time you are having dinner with a group of friends, try leaving your phone at home.

Make It Work for You

A digital detox can be whatever you want it to be and can take many forms. You might want to try giving up all digital devices for a time, including television, mobile phones, and social media. In other cases, you might want to focus on restricting your use of just one type of digital device such as your phone or your gaming console.

Some ideas that you might consider trying:

A digital fast: Try giving up all digital devices for a short period of time, such as a day or up to a week

Recurrent digital abstinence: Pick one day of the week to go device-free

A specific detox: If one app, site, game, or digital tool is taking up too much of your time, focus on restricting your use of that problematic item

A social media detox: Focus on restricting or even completely eliminating your social media use for a specific period of time

Digital Detox Tips

Some people find giving up their devices fairly easy. Others will find it much more difficult and even anxiety-provoking at times.

There are some things that you can do to ensure that your digital detox is more successful:

Let your friends and family know that you are on a digital detox and ask for their help and support

Find ways to stay distracted and keep other activities on hand

Delete social media apps from your phone to reduce temptation and easy access

Try getting out of the house; go to dinner with friends or go for a walk when you are tempted to use your device

Keep a journal to track your progress and write down your thoughts about the experience

Going device-free can be uncomfortable and stressful at times. You might feel annoyed, anxious, and even bored without your mobile phone and other tech tools. While it may be hard, it can be a rewarding experience that will help you better understand your relationship with your devices and be more present and mindful in your other activities and experiences.

HOW TO DO A DOPAMINE DETOX OR DOPAMINE FAST

First understand that there is no one "right way" to do this, each approach will be different for different people. This is because we each have our own crosses to bear and what does "it" for one person, might not be right for you.

Every part of modern society, social media, and our phones are optimized to give us the rewarding feeling of dopamine hits, but these are fleeting and surface level.

To make this a bit easier to understand I want to explain this with a conceptual framework I'm calling behavior "loops". Essentially a behavior loop is a behavior cycle where we experience a trigger, we decide to respond to it with an action, that action triggers a response, and then that action is reinforced. We have "escape loops" and we have "engagement loops".

Escape Loops: Shortcuts To Happiness That Leave Us Miserable

Escape loops are essentially things in our lives that provide us with low value pleasures. They are characterized by a big hit of dopamine, that's quick, easy and cheap to attain. The "loop" of escapes loops typically breaks down to something like this:

Escape loops offer a way to side step the root cause of the problem and just skip to feeling good, even if it's a shallow pleasure. We essentially sacrifice our future well-being by avoiding the real problem all for a cheap dopamine hit. Looking at it in this manner, it's similar to how drug users operate: feel bad, instead of fixing the issue they seek a high, then come down to only feel worse. At its core, an escape loop is a self-sabotaging behavior.

Some examples would be: When we feel bored, instead of developing hobbies, we pick up our phone. When we feel anxious about a difficult conversation that we need to have with the person we are dating, we ghost them and move on to a new person. If we are miserable at work, instead of seeking a new opportunity, we have a few beers or glasses of wine each night to forget it all. Rather than going on dates to meet someone new, we pull up a website and watch a video to get off. Escape loops are different for each person.

ENGAGEMENT LOOPS: FIXING THE CORE ISSUES FOR LONG TERM CONTENTMENT

Engagement Loops are essentially the opposite of escape loops. Instead of seeking quick hits of dopamine, we delay gratification to build a deeper and richer life for ourselves over time. If we don't make this conscious choice, we fall into the trappings of modern society that have been designed to reward us in ways that are advantageous to those who want to capture our attention for their own benefit.

Engagement behaviors are often the difficult road, the things we know we should do, but don't really want to do. I know after a long day, the last thing I want to do is leave the comfort zone of my home and hit the gym, meet up with friends or go on a date.

Sometimes the choices seem trivial: order a water or a diet soda at dinner. Our friend is a few minutes late, do we pull out our phone or take a minute to reflect on the day. The truth is, a good life is built on a strong foundation of small positive actions taken over and over again, it is the aggregate of these "trivial" things that actually make a good life. I once heard a top Olympic athlete say he visualized the little actions like laying a single stone, each one building his castle.

Engagement loops are difficult work that requires dedication and effort, but results in an outcome that is deeply meaningful. Engagement loops build lasting change that leads to a life worth living. After much reflection on this, I believe that engagement loops build fulfillment, answering the greatest question of them all, arguably the most important question: what is the meaning of life? Engagement loops are different for each person.

Think about the challenges you face in life, the shortcomings you have as a person, and the long list of failures in your past. Analyze these symptoms and try to discern what the root causes are, these are the things you need to counter, because they are the things you try to avoid dealing with when you seek an escape loop.

I recommend focusing on one main escape loop at a time, but layering a few positive engagement loops to replace it. The reason for this being they provide a big hit of dopamine over a very short period of time, similar to how our brain reacts to narcotics.

Compare that to something like eating a healthy diet, at first there is not a whole lot of reward, but over a long period you see the benefits. It's no wonder that getting a lot of "likes" on your latest social post feels better than getting dressed, driving through traffic, and paying $10 for a drink to have a conversation with someone you just met for the first time.; At first, receiving the "likes" feels better but the long-term implications tell a different story.

It is for this reason I suggest you replace your worst escape loop with many engagement loops to have any hope of making the change stick. If we layer in these positive forces, their high-quality dopamine hits will overpower the cheap easy thrills of our vices.

WHAT ARE THE DOPAMINE DETOX RULES?

There are no hard and fast rules and it depends on how long you plan to detox. While it can be nice to do a deep detox where you totally cut things out, most of this might only be able to do this for a single weekend. I hold the belief that quick fixes fall prey to the same faults that surround our escapes.

24 Hour Dopamine Detox Rules

Some people like to try a short 24 hour fast, though the impact of this will be minimal, unless followed up with a prolonged detox which strikes the balance of you needing to handle daily life while keeping the big offenders at bay. Here is a general list of rules for a 24-hour dopamine detox:

i. no electrics of any kind (phone, tv, computer, video games, etc)

ii. no reading of books, newspapers, magazines

iii. no sex or masturbation

iv. no talking

v. no food (consult doctor but drink water)

vi. no music, podcasts, tv or movies)

vii. no coffee or other stimulants)

30 DAY DOPAMINE FAST

Most of us can't run off to a mountain top and live like a cloistered monk for several months, so we need to take a more measured approach and, if truth be told, this is going to be more effective. seeking a quick fix is an escape loop in and of itself!

Additionally, we need to be able to live and operate in society, we have to be able to contend with the pulls of modernity, so we must struggle to find our paths despite these things. To effectively replace negative loops, we need to slowly reinforce our new positive habits over time.

Start by choosing one of your bigger escape loops that feed your dopaminergic system in a negative way and define engagement loops to replace it. Use the above questions about escape and engagement loops to determine what your particular burden is, think about how this impacts your life, then determine what positive actions should be used to replace it. For Example: if you dread your work, instead of complaining about it and drinking a few too many glasses of wine. Commit to polishing up your resume, set a goal to take an interview per month and when you feel the stress of work, instead of popping a cork, go outside for a walk.

You want to try to choose negative loops and positive loops that have symmetry to them. Understand the root cause of your discontent and dopamine seeking behavior, then develop a related counter to it. We want to train ourselves to recognize when we are reaching for that escape loop behavior and then replace it with one of our engagement loops. This gradually will disincentivize our negative behaviors and build a positive feedback loop for our good ones.

Each person should figure out which escape and engagement loops apply to their lives, because it will be specific to each individual. Here are some general tips I suggest during your 30+ day detox:

> Turn off all the badge icons and notifications on your phone, set it to silent
> Uninstall all social media, dating and work apps from your phone
> When you're doing work, close your email screen and turn off notifications
> Try doing only one task at a time, avoid multi-tasking
> Make sure you spend time outside each day
> Try meditating, even if it's only for a few minutes
> Be present with your friends, family and romantic partners, put down the phone
> Consider doing some journaling exercises
> Drink water each day

Take these as suggestions, each person is going to need something different. Just be honest with yourself and realize that replacing these behaviors requires hard work, self-discipline and effort on your part.

HOW LONG DOES IT TAKE TO ADJUST DOPAMINE LEVELS?

This is a complicated question, but in general it can take an average of 66 days to build a new habit. The brutal thing is that bad habits can take root much faster and it can take a long time to build good ones.

Dopamine levels change from minute to minute as our bodies react to the world around us, as I pointed out above, the title of "dopamine detox" or "dopamine fast" is a bit of a misnomer. We always have dopamine; it's always reacting and too little or too much can be bad for our health. We shouldn't really try to control our dopamine levels, just the behaviors we choose to engage with that might act as levers for dopamine.

HOW DOPAMINE AFFECTS OUR BEHAVIOR

One of the most prominent neurotransmitters that impact human behavior is dopamine. When we experience pleasurable events like eating satisfying food, sexual activity, or drug use, our body releases dopamine. Our brain then associates the release of dopamine with pleasure and creates a reward system. For example, when you eat comforting food, your brain releases dopamine, which makes you feel good. Therefore, your brain assumes this is a reward and encourages you to repeat this behavior, even though the comforting food may not be the healthiest choice for your body.

Dopamine is associated with reinforcement. It is thought to be the chemical that motivates a person to do something repeatedly. Reward and reinforcement help us create our personal habits. Humans gravitate toward positive experiences and avoid negative ones. Dopamine is what drives us to create these patterns. This is why people with low dopamine levels may be more likely to develop addictions to drugs, food, sex, or alcohol.

DOPAMINE AND MENTAL HEALTH

Dopamine deficiency can have adverse physical and psychological effects

It is important to note that abnormally low levels of dopamine are not only associated with addiction but can cause physical and mental impairments because this major body chemical controls many body functions.

Low dopamine has been linked to impairments such as:

- Anxiety
- Addiction
- Behavioral disturbances
- Brain fog
- Mental health disorders
- Mood swings
- Delusional behavior
- Depression
- Feelings of hopelessness
- Low self-esteem

- Lack of motivation
- Suicidal thoughts or thoughts of self-harm
- Low sex drive
- Psychosis

A release of dopamine is what tells the brain whether an experience was pleasurable enough to experience again. When there is a lack of dopamine, it can cause people to change their behaviors in ways that will help release more of this chemical. They will pursue activities that trigger their reward center, even if these activities are harmful or taboo. They may seek illicit drugs or alcohol or engage in other harmful, addictive behaviors. An imbalance of dopamine can create an unhealthy reward system response in the brain.

LACK OF SLEEP MAY LOWER DOPAMINE LEVELS

Lack of dopamine can make you sleepy — but not sleeping may also lower your dopamine.

One small study in 2012Trusted Source suggests that sleep deprivation can lead to a noticeable reduction in the availability of dopamine receptors in the morning.

Conditions associated with low dopamine levels

Some conditions that may be associated with low dopamine are:

Parkinson's disease; symptoms include tremors, slowed movement, and sometimes psychosis.

Depression; symptoms include sadness, sleep problems, and cognitive changes.

Dopamine transporter deficiency syndrome; also known as infantile parkinsonism-dystonia, this condition causes movement abnormalities similar to those of Parkinson's disease.

What happens when you have too much dopamine?

Very high levels of dopamine can make you feel on top of the world, at least for a while. It can also put you into serious overdrive.

In excess, it may be a contributing factor in:

> mania
> hallucinations
> delusions
> Too much dopamine may play a role in:
> obesity
> addiction
> schizophrenia

How do drugs affect dopamine levels?

Certain drugs may interact with dopamine in a way that becomes habit-forming.

Nicotine, alcohol, or other drugs with addictive qualities activate the dopamine cycle.

These substances can cause a quicker, far more intense dopamine rush than you'd get from those double chocolate chip cookies. It's such a powerful rush that you're left wanting more — and soon.

As a habit forms, the brain responds by toning down the dopamine. Now you need more of the substance to get to that same pleasure level.

Overactivation also affects dopamine receptors in a way that makes you lose interest in other things. That can make you act more compulsively. You're less and less able to resist using these substances.

When it becomes more of a need than a want, this is addiction. If you try to stop, you might go through physical and emotional symptoms of withdrawal.

Even if you've stopped using the substances for a long time, exposure to the substance may trigger your desire and put you at risk of relapsing.

Dopamine doesn't bear sole responsibility for creating addiction. Other things, like genetics and environmental factors, play a role.

How do hormones affect dopamine levels?

Dopamine also interacts with other neurotransmitters and hormones. For example, the neurotransmitter glutamate is involved in the pleasure and reward cycle in the brain.

Various sources looked at how stress and sex hormones affect dopamine neurotransmission during adolescence.

The researchers noted that testosterone, estrogen, and glucocorticoids interact with each other and impact dopamine levels. This can affect brain maturation and cognitive function in adolescence and into adulthood.

A 2015 study from a Trusted Source noted that neurotransmitters are affected by many things. The researchers wrote that sex hormones are "highly intertwined" with:

- dopamine
- serotonin
- GABA
- glutamate

These interactions are complicated and not entirely understood. More research is needed to fully understand how dopamine interacts with other neurotransmitters and hormones.

Key takeaways

Dopamine's claim to fame comes from its effect on mood and pleasure, as well as the motivation-reward-reinforcement cycle.

We know that dopamine serves many vital neurological and cognitive functions. Despite a lot of research, there's still much to learn about dopamine's interactions with other neurotransmitters and hormones.

See your doctor if you have movement abnormalities, symptoms of a mood disorder, or believe you're experiencing addiction.

THE RELATIONSHIP OF DOPAMINE TO SUBSTANCE ABUSE

The genetics department of the University of Utah explains, "all addictive drugs affect brain pathways involving reward — that is, the dopamine system in the reward pathway." The impact that drugs and alcohol have on the natural reward center is more intense than is naturally found in the body. This over-stimulation may, according to university researchers, "decrease the brain's response to natural rewards" and may result in a person's inability to feel pleasure except as triggered by the abused substance.

Because dopamine is the chemical that drives us to seek positive experiences and avoid negative ones, when this reward system is damaged, human behavior patterns may change to seek out harmful situations and substances as a means of pleasure.

Going from a low dopamine state to a high dopamine state due to the use of illicit drugs is one example of how a person can damage their cognitive function. Though drug use is harmful, the brain only recognizes that it is a source of pleasure and does not seek to stop the behavior. The person's mind now sees drug use as a pleasurable experience, even if this is an irrational choice for their overall health.

The brain may view many negative experiences as positive ones when its reward system has been damaged. This is true not only with drug use but also in situations such as trauma bonding, where a person stays in a relationship regardless of how harmful or abusive it may be. Though the reality of the interaction with this person may be damaging, the brain does not recognize it as such. This is a clear example of how powerful brain chemicals can be.

Addictive Personality Theory

Some scientists have coined the term "addictive personality theory." This theory supports the premise that certain personality types are more likely to become addicted to drugs or alcohol, depending on factors such as genetics and biochemical makeup. However, other researchers suggest that factors such as early exposure to illicit drugs, familial support, and socioeconomic status can impact a person's likelihood of becoming addicted.

Mental health issues may also correspond with a higher risk of addiction. Research suggests that people with mental health conditions may be more likely to abuse mind-altering substances. Some researchers believe that those with a mental health diagnosis, such as schizophrenia or attention deficit hyperactivity disorder, are more likely to turn to illicit drugs to "self-treat" their disorder.

Does Increased Risk of Addiction Lie within our DNA?

There is much debate in the current medical community as to whether addiction is a choice or a disease, and whether low dopamine might be a contributing cause for addiction. Some in the addiction medicine community believe that certain people are more genetically predisposed to addiction, suggesting that a person's likelihood of addiction lies within their DNA. Every individual responds to substances differently. For example, some people become intoxicated very easily, while others can withstand higher amounts of alcohol before getting drunk. Differences like these may be influenced by variations in genetic makeup.

Genetic variants associated with these types of responses are central to the argument for the "genetic predisposition to addiction" theory. This theory suggests that substance abuse can run in families because of an underlying inherited component.

Symptoms of Low Dopamine

It is obvious that dopamine plays a major role in how humans behave. Low amounts of this neurotransmitter can negatively impact a person's quality of life. Dopamine levels impact mood regulation, muscle movement, sleep patterns, ability to store and recall memories, concentration, appetite, and ability to express self-control. When there is an imbalance in this chemical, a person cannot function at an optimal level.

Possible symptoms of low dopamine may include but are not limited to:

- Aches and pains
- Difficulty swallowing
- Tremors
- Muscle spasms
- Stiffness/difficulty moving
- Loss of balance
- Disturbed sleep patterns (such as insomnia or excessive sleeping)

It is important to note that everyone is different and may not exhibit the same symptoms. If you suspect you or someone you care for may have a dopamine deficiency, there are many ways your healthcare provider can help.

Neurotransmitter testing can identify specific biochemical imbalances. A neurotransmitter panel can check the levels of brain chemicals such as dopamine, serotonin, GABA, glutamate, epinephrine, and norepinephrine.

An astute doctor will most likely run a series of tests to accurately gauge any deficiencies you may have. Neurotransmitters are one of the principal factors that can impact your life. With the help of a knowledgeable healthcare team, you can regain control of your health.

DOPAMINE AND ADDICTION: SEPARATING MYTHS AND FACTS

The involvement of dopamine in drug reinforcement is well recognized but its role in drug addiction is much less clear. Imaging studies have shown that the reinforcing effects of drugs of abuse in humans are contingent upon large and fast increases in dopamine that mimic but exceed in the intensity and duration those induced by dopamine cell firing to environmental events. In addition, imaging studies have also documented a role of dopamine in motivation, which appears to be encoded both by fast as well as smooth DA increases. Since dopamine cells fire in response to salient stimuli, the supraphysiological activation by drugs is likely to be experienced as highly salient (driving attention, arousal conditioned learning and motivation) and may also reset the thresholds required for environmental events to activate dopamine cells. Indeed, imaging studies have shown that in drug-addicted subjects, dopamine function is markedly disrupted (decreases in dopamine release and in dopamine D2 receptors in striatum) and this is associated with reduced activity of the orbitofrontal cortex (neuroanatomical region involved with salience attribution and motivation and implicated in compulsive behaviors) and the cingulate gyrus (neuroanatomical region involved with inhibitory control and attention and implicated in impulsivity). However, when addicted subjects are exposed to drug-related stimuli, these hypoactive regions become hyperactive in proportion to the expressed desire for the drug. We postulate that decreased dopamine function in addicted subjects results in decreased sensitivity to nondrug-related stimuli (including natural reinforcers) and disrupts frontal inhibition, both of which contribute to compulsive drug intake and impaired inhibitory control. These findings suggest new strategies for pharmacological and behavioral treatments, which focus on enhancing DA function and restoring brain circuits disrupted by chronic drug use to help motivate the addicted subject in activities that provide alternative sources of reinforcement, counteract conditioned responses, enhance their ability to control their drive to take drugs and interfere with their compulsive administration.

You've probably heard of dopamine as a "pleasure chemical" that's been associated with addiction.

Think of the term "dopamine rush." People use it to describe the flood of pleasure that comes from making a new purchase or finding a $20 bill on the ground.

But some of what you've heard may be more myth than fact.

Experts are still studying exactly how dopamine, a neurotransmitter, works in the context of addiction. Many believe it trains your brain to avoid unpleasant experiences and seek out pleasurable ones.

It's this role in reinforcing your brain's quest for pleasure that's led many to associate dopamine with addiction. But it's not that simple. While dopamine does play a role in addiction, this role is complex and not fully understood.

Myth: You can be addicted to dopamine

There's a popular misconception that people experiencing addiction are actually addicted to dopamine, rather than drugs or certain activities.

Experiences that make you feel good, including using drugs, activate your brain's reward center, which responds by releasing dopamine. This release causes your brain to focus more of its attention on the experience. As a result, you're left with a strong memory of the pleasure you felt.

This strong memory can prompt you to make an effort to experience it again by using drugs or seeking out certain experiences. But the drug or activity is still the underlying source of this behavior.

Fact: Dopamine is a motivator

While dopamine isn't the sole cause of addiction, its motivational properties are thought to play a role in addiction.

Remember, the reward center in your brain releases dopamine in response to pleasurable experiences. This part of your brain is also closely linked to memory and motivation.

THE SEEDS OF ADDICTION

Generally speaking, when you experience a positive sensation and dopamine is released into the pathways of the reward center, your brain takes note of:

What triggered the sensation: Was it a substance? A behavior? A type of food?

Any cues from your environment that can help you find it again. Did you experience it at night? What else were you doing? Were you with a certain person?

When you're exposed to those environmental cues, you'll begin to feel the same drive to seek out that same pleasure. This drive can be incredibly powerful, creating an urge that's hard to control.

Keep in mind that this process doesn't always involve harmful substances or activities.

Eating good food, having sex, creating art, and a range of other things can trigger similar responses from your brain's reward center.

Myth: Dopamine is the 'pleasure chemical'

People sometimes refer to dopamine as the "pleasure chemical." This term stems from the misconception that dopamine is directly responsible for feelings of euphoria or pleasure.

Dopamine does contribute to your experience of pleasure. But it doesn't have much to do with creating pleasurable feelings, experts believe.

Instead, it helps reinforce enjoyable sensations and behaviors by linking things that make you feel good with a desire to do them again. This link is an important factor in the development of addiction.

Neurotransmitters that do cause feelings of pleasure or euphoria include:

➢ serotonin
➢ endorphins
➢ oxytocin

Fact: Dopamine plays a role in developing tolerance

In the context of drugs, tolerance refers to the point at which you stop feeling the effects of a drug to the same degree that you used to, even though you're consuming the same amount of the drug.

If you develop a tolerance to a substance, you'll need to use more of it to feel the effects you're used to. Dopamine plays a role in this process.

Consistent drug misuse eventually leads to overstimulation in the reward center. Its pathways become overwhelmed, making it harder for it to handle the high levels of dopamine being released.

The brain tries to solve this problem in two ways:

❖ decreasing dopamine production
❖ reducing dopamine receptors

Either change generally results in the substance having less of an effect due to a weaker response by the brain's reward center.

Still, the craving to use remains. It just takes more of the drug to satisfy it.

There's no single cause of addiction

Addiction is a complex brain disorder that doesn't have a single, obvious cause. Dopamine plays a role, but it's one small piece of a larger puzzle.

Experts believe a range of biological and environmental factors can significantly increase someone's risk for addiction.

Some of these biological factors include:

Genes. According to the National Institute on Drug Abuse, about 40 to 60 percent of addiction risk stems from genetic factors.

Health history. Having a history of certain medical conditions, particularly mental health conditions, can increase your risk.

Developmental stage. According to the Centers for Disease Control and Prevention source, using drugs as a teenager increases your risk for addiction down the road.

Environmental factors, particularly for children and teenagers, include:

Home life. Living with or near people who misuse drugs can increase risk.

Social influences. Having friends who take drugs can make it more likely you'll try them and potentially develop an addiction.

Challenges at school. Having troubles socially or academically can increase your risk for trying drugs and eventually developing an addiction.

These are just some of the many factors that can contribute to addiction. Keep in mind they don't mean an addiction will definitely develop.

The bottom line

Dopamine is one of the many factors that can contribute to addiction. Contrary to popular belief, you can't be addicted dopamine. But it does play an important role in motivating you to seek out pleasurable experiences.

Dopamine also contributes to tolerance, which requires you to need more of a substance or activity to feel the same effects you initially did.

WHAT IS THE CONNECTION BETWEEN DOPAMINE AND PARKINSON'S DISEASE?

Parkinson's disease is a complex motor disorder that can cause unintentional or uncontrollable movements. It typically occurs due to low levels of dopamine in the brain. Dopamine is a chemical that plays an important role in movement and coordination.

Parkinson's disease (PD) is a progressive disorder that develops due to the degeneration of nerve cells in the brain that control movement. Normally, dopamine and other neurotransmitters work together to help coordinate movement. But without sufficient dopamine, this is not possible.

Estimates are that roughly 1.5 million people in the United States currently have Parkinson's disease, with approximately 60,000 American people receiving a diagnosis each year.

In this page, we will discuss the role of dopamine in Parkinson's disease, as well as symptoms, diagnosis, and treatment options for the condition.

About Parkinson's disease

Parkinson's disease is a neurodegenerative disorder of the nervous system that affects movement and worsens over time.

The condition occurs due to damage or death of nerve cells, or neurons, in an area of the brain called the substantia nigra. This part of the brain plays a critical role in controlling movement.

Neurons in the substantia nigra are dopaminergic. This means they are responsible for producing dopamine. If they are unable to produce dopamine, a person will likely begin to experience movement-related problems, such as tremors, rigidity, slowness of movement, and poor balance, which are all symptoms of Parkinson's disease.

Role of dopamine in the disease

Dopamine is an important neurotransmitter that plays a critical role in a number of bodily functions, such as movement and coordination. As such, low dopamine levels can cause problems with movement.

Dopamine is the chemical messenger that transmits signals between the substantia nigra and the corpus striatum. Researchers may refer to this as the nigrostriatal pathway. Both the substantia nigra and corpus striatum form part of the basal ganglia, which is a group of structures in the brain that help facilitate movement.

Low levels of dopamine may disrupt the nigrostriatal pathway and cause abnormal nerve firing patterns, which can result in movement problems. Evidence suggests that most people with PD lose 60–80% or more of dopamine-producing cells in the substantia nigra by the time they present symptoms.

Symptoms

The four main symptoms of PD include:

Tremor: This refers to the shaking a person with PD may experience. It often begins in a hand but can start in a foot or the jaw. It features a characteristic rhythmic back-and-forth motion and is most obvious at rest or when under stress. It may also disappear during sleep.

Rigidity: This refers to muscle stiffness or difficulty moving. Often, the muscles remain constantly tense, which may cause a person to feel stiff or achy.

Bradykinesia: This refers to slow or difficult movement, which can make performing simple tasks difficult. This may mean that routine activities such as washing or dressing now take much longer.

Postural instability: Changes in posture and poor balance can increase the risk of falls and potential injuries.

People may not experience PD the same way, and the progression of the condition may also differ among individuals.

Early symptoms may be subtle and occur gradually. People may experience mild tremors, start noticing difficulty moving, or realize that tasks begin to take longer to complete. Some may notice that symptoms begin on one side of the body but eventually affect both sides. Symptoms are often less severe on one side than the other.

As the condition progresses, symptoms may start to interfere more with daily tasks. People may notice that shaking makes it very difficult for them to eat, they struggle getting out of a seat, and they may speak too softly or with hesitation.

Causes

Researchers are still unsure on the precise cause of PD. At present, evidence suggests that it most likely results from a combination of genetics and exposure to environmental factors that trigger the condition.

Scientists have identified that PD occurs when neurons in the brain become impaired or die and start producing less dopamine. However, they are unclear exactly what causes this. The National Institute of Neurological Disorders and Stroke suggests the following potential causes:

Genetics: Several genetic mutations appear to have links with PD. However, researchers do not consider the condition to be hereditary. Research suggests that genetic factors may only account for roughly 10% of cases.

Environment: Exposure to certain toxins, such as MPTP or manganese, may result in the development of PD. There may also be many other environmental factors that may contribute to the condition in genetically susceptible individuals.

Lewy bodies: A person with PD may have deposits of a protein called alpha-synuclein in their brain. Experts may refer to this protein clump as Lewy bodies. The accumulation of these proteins may cause the degeneration of neurons that typically results in PD.

Mitochondria: Many people may refer to mitochondria as the powerhouses of the cell. Some research indicates that mitochondrial dysfunction may cause the neurodegeneration that results in PD.

Diagnosis

Currently, there is no specific test for PD. A doctor may diagnose PD based on:

> ➢ a neurological exam and medical history
> ➢ blood and other laboratory tests
> ➢ brain scans
> ➢ Some diagnostic tests a doctor may perform include:

DaTscan: This is an imaging technique that determines how much dopamine is available in a person's brain. It is a specific type of nuclear medicine called single photon emission computed tomography (SPECT).

MRI or CT scan: These other scans can rule out a stroke or brain tumor, which may cause similar symptoms.

Blood tests: A doctor may suggest a blood test to rule out other possible causes, such as liver damage or abnormal thyroid hormone levels.

Levodopa test: Levodopa (L-Dopa)Trusted Source is the precursor to dopamine and a drug that can boost dopamine levels. If a person displays improved symptoms after taking L-Dopa, it indicates a diagnosis of PD.

BRAIN'S DOPAMINE: THE GOOD, THE BAD AND THE UGLY

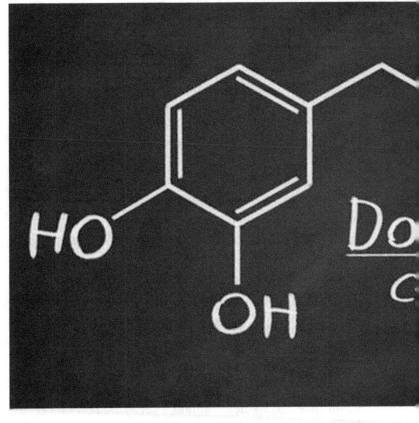

You set out a goal for a game, and you achieved it. Apart from the cheerleaders in the arena, there is an internal cheerleader who makes you happy and gives you that motivated feeling. That is Dopamine. Dopamine in the brain is an important neurotransmitter that is often attributed to pleasure chemical. But that's not all it does; research has identified the role of dopamine in fear, emotion and risk perception also. Just like it can motivate you to do more, it can also make you do less.

Too much of good is also dangerous, and one primary example is an addiction. Feeling of being high is due to the dopamine release during the rewarding experiences, and if one seeks out those pleasurable experiences regularly, that's an addiction.

Also, both healthy and unhealthy cues modulate dopamine levels, and our body responds in various ways to balance it — the balance of dopamine levels in often termed as good health. Low levels of dopamine lead to an inability to feel pleasure, like in depression. Other problems associated with dopamine deficiency are fatigue, forgetfulness, obesity, trouble concentrating and difficulty in completing tasks. On the other side, excess dopamine is also bad as too much is associated with schizophrenia and psychosis.

With dopamine release in both desire and dread, it sure seems to be a boon and a bane. This double-edged sword sure does intrigue many scientists to investigate further. A 2018 study by researchers from the University of California, Berkeley, found yet another facet of Dopamine. The critical finding published in Neuron is that dopamine is also released in response to unpleasurable experiences, to prime the brain for future avoidance behavior.

"In addiction, people only look for the next reward, and they will take a lot of risks to get the next shot of drugs of abuse," said Stephan Lammel, a UC Berkeley assistant professor of molecular and cell biology and the senior author of a paper describing the results in the journal Neuron. "We currently do not know the neurobiological underpinnings of certain high-risk behaviors of individuals with addiction, such as sharing drug paraphernalia despite the proven risk of mortality and morbidity associated with it. An understanding of how drugs change neural circuits involved in aversion may have important implications for the persistent nature of drug-seeking behavior in the face of negative consequences."

Although some neuroscientists have long speculated about dopamine's potential role in the signaling of aversive events, its dual personality remained hidden until recently because the neurons in the brain that release dopamine in response to rewards is embedded in a different subcircuit than the neurons that release dopamine in response to aversive stimuli.

Johannes de Jong, the first author of the study, was able to simultaneously record from both dopamine subcircuits by implanting fiber optic cannulas in two brain regions—separated by just a few millimeters—using a new technology called fiber photometry.

"Our work delineates for the first time the precise brain circuitry in which learning about rewarding and aversive outcomes occurs," Lammel said. "Having separate neuronal correlates for appetitive and aversive behavior in our brain may explain why we are striving for ever-greater rewards while simultaneously minimizing threats and dangers. Such balanced behavior of approach-and-avoidance learning is surely helpful for surviving competition in a constantly changing environment."

The newly discovered role for dopamine aligns with an increasing recognition that the neurotransmitter has entirely different roles in different areas of the brain, exemplified by its function involuntary movement, which is affected in Parkinson's disease. The results also explain earlier conflicting experiments, some of which showed that dopamine increases in response to aversive stimuli, while others did not.

"We have moved away from considering dopamine neurons as just a homogeneous cell population in the brain that mediates reward and pleasure to a more defined, nuanced picture of the role of dopamine, depending on where it is released in the brain," Lammel said.

Most of what is known about dopamine has been inferred from studies in rodents and monkeys, where researchers recorded from cells in a specific region of the brain that only contains reward-responsive dopamine neurons. It is possible, Lammel said, that through sampling biases, dopamine neurons that respond to aversive stimulation had been missed.

According to the reigning "reward prediction error hypothesis," dopamine neurons are activated and produce dopamine when an action is more rewarding than we expect, but they remain at baseline activity when the reward matches our expectations and show depressed activity when we receive less reward than predicted.

Dopamine changes neural circuits and trains the brain—for better or worse—to pursue the pleasurable and avoid the unpleasurable.

"Based on the reward prediction error hypothesis, the established tendency has been to emphasize dopamine involvement in reward, pleasure, addiction and reward-related learning, with less consideration of the involvement of dopamine in aversive processes," Lammel said.

To dissect the different dopamine subcircuits, de Jong and Lammel collaborated with the laboratory of Karl Deisseroth at Stanford University, who developed the fiber photometry technology a few years ago.

Fiber photometry involves threading thin, flexible fiber-optic wires into the brain and recording fluorescent signals given off by neurons and their axons that release dopamine. The fluorescent markers are inserted into the neurons via a virus that targets only these cells.

In previous experiments in monkeys, Lammel said, scientists had recorded from dopamine cells without knowing where in the brain the cells' axons reached, which could be areas millimeters from the cell body. Working with mice, de Jong recorded simultaneously from dopamine axons in the lateral and medial regions of an area called the nucleus accumbens, considered an integral part of the brain's reward circuits. He thus captured the activity of cells whose axons reach into these regions from the dopamine areas in the midbrain, specifically the ventral tegmental area.

To their surprise, axons in the medial area released dopamine in response to an aversive stimulus—a mild electrical shock to the foot—while those in the lateral area released dopamine only after positive stimuli.

"We have two different subtypes of dopamine cells: one population mediates attraction, and one mediates aversion, and they are anatomically separated," Lammel said.

He hopes that these findings can be confirmed in monkeys and humans, and lead to new approaches to understanding and treating addiction and other brain maladies.

The dopamine released when you read the beginning sure will motivate you to continue this e-book, (laughs).

DOES A DOPAMINE DETOX HAVE BENEFITS?

Research shows that fasting, whether religious or not, can have several health benefits.

For example, a study published in the Journal of Research in Medical Science had 14 individuals undergo a 10-day silent Vipassana meditation retreat. The participants reported significant improvements in physical and psychological well-being after the fast.

According to a research review by nutrition scientists John Trepanowski and Richard Bloomer, religious and nonreligious fasting can have similar health benefits.

Dopamine fasting is supposed to make ordinary tasks such as eating and listening to music more pleasurable. After temporarily abstaining from an activity, fasters have found it more rewarding to reengage in the activity.

There are those who disagree. Neuroscientists have argued that dopamine is essential to healthy brain functioning and have raised questions about the trend's apparent goal of reducing dopamine.

While it is true that certain behaviors lead to the increase of dopamine, experts caution on the claims regarding dopamine fasting. Joshua Berke, a neuroscientist, said that dopamine is not a "pleasure juice" with a certain level that gets depleted. Rather, the dynamic of dopamine changes from moment to moment.

Nonetheless, advocates of dopamine fasting believe that it can curb addictive behaviors and make daily life more pleasurable, something that religious traditions have for millennia encouraged people to develop – patterns of fasting and feasting.

We have already clarified that a complete and total detox from naturally-occurring dopamine is not possible.

That said, the decision to unplug and detach from certain impulsive behaviors may come with some health benefits, one of which is the potential for heightened focus and greater mental clarity.

Dopamine is often distracting, and may be a hindrance for some people from achieving their goals. It is what prompts the excessive repetition of certain feel-good behaviors, causing people to scroll mindlessly on social media or binge-watch their favorite TV shows.

These unnecessary compulsions detract from spending time more productively on work, health goals, home organization, and more. When people actively avoid these distractions, they may free up more time for the things that matter more to them.

In short, a dopamine detox is not technically possible, and any evidence of its positive effects are purely anecdotal.

However, by avoiding certain behaviors, such as spending hours scrolling through a smartphone and social media sites, people may be able to achieve a greater state of mindfulness, which comes with its own benefits. Among these are stress relief, lower blood pressure, and improved sleep.

Benefits:

Benefits of Dopamine Fa

- Increased ability to focus on har tasks.
- Increased self-motivation.
- Improved emotion regulation.
- Developed greater self-control ar willpower.
- Developed and improved patienc
- Grater life satisfaction.
- A real sense of fulfilment.
- Increased feelings of self-worth.
- Developed solid self-discipline.
- Being achievement oriented.
- Having the right priorities.

Calm Sage

1. Increases ability to focus

With the help of dopamine fasting, you can increase your capability of focus. As dopamine fasting is related to the idea of less stress and distractions. This can happen by bringing some positive alterations to your everyday lifestyle.

2. Increases self-motivation

As dopamine fasting improves focus, it directly increases self-motivation and this self-motivation helps in increasing daily productivity. Dopamine fasting overall benefits our everyday lifestyle and also helps in achieving the main focus of our goals and career.

3. Improves emotional regulation

Dopamine fasting improves emotional regulation because we tend to stay distant from social services and other toxicity which helps in attaining emotional regulation and it also helps in bringing peace again in our lives.

4. Develops great self-control and willpower

With the help of dopamine fasting, we maintain distance from the real world and social media. This helps in developing great self-control and willpower as this type of fasting is related to mindfulness-based activities.

5. Develops and improves patience

Dopamine fasting is related to mindfulness activities which helps to develop and increase and patience levels. If we practice it 4-5 hours before sleeping, it will improve our patience and as well as sleeping cycle.

6. Increases life satisfaction

When we start living with peaceful and stress-free life, it eventually increases the satisfaction towards life. Dopamine fasting basically takes us out from stress and brings back us to peace by distancing us from a toxic and stressful world.

The idea is to have fewer distractions and stress. This can only happen by minimizing distractions in our lifestyles.

For example, if you start practicing dopamine fasting for 3-4 hours a day before sleep, it can actually work in a positive way. These practices are more like mindfulness-based activities that reduce stress as well. Hence, dopamine fasting helps in refraining from unhealthy habits.

COMMON QUESTIONS RELATED TO DOPAMINE FASTING

1. Is it Possible to Control Naturally Occurring Brain Chemicals?

During the events of pleasure, motivation, reward, and learning the dopamine does rise. But, whenever we try to avoid compulsive behaviors in order to control dopamine, it doesn't actually lower the dopamine levels. Some people take it as a "tolerance break" by depriving themselves of pleasure, but when you consume it again, it will be more intense. Therefore, it is hard to say if dopamine fast could help control dopamine levels.

2. Does Dopamine Fasting Help Relax the Mind?

Yes, you can try dopamine fast for short durations from one hour to four hours at the end of the day to take a much-needed break to calm your mind and relax your body. As fasting is in practice for hundreds of years, dopamine fasting is another method of mindfulness practice.

But, if you completely refrain from eating for long hours, or avoid socializing, or listening to music, or engaging yourself in pleasurable tasks, it is not going to as a positive outcome. In fact, misunderstanding the concept of dopamine fasting can create maladaptive behavior which might affect your day-to-day life.

3. Does Dopamine Fasting Help Cure Technology Addiction?

Talking about the actual intention behind dopamine fasting, dopamine fasting was introduced to disconnect yourself from tech-frenzy activities so that you can spare time for yourself. The concept was to reconnect with ourselves and others, doing small important things in life, and stay happy.

While the idea is worthwhile, healthy, and noble, it is not the complete solution. At the same time, it gives you a direction to lead a stress-free life where technology isn't following you. At least for a few hours a day!

4. Is Dopamine Fasting Going to Stay Longer?

Fasting isn't a new trend, instead people are fasting for a long, the only difference is dopamine fasting is related to curbing screen-time. So, technically yes, dopamine fasting is going to stay longer. As people are more dependent on tech devices, they would definitely need a break from it at least for some time.

CONCLUSION

The misunderstood version of the "dopamine detox" is little more than a fad, with no scientific evidence to support its effectiveness.

A true "dopamine detox" is impossible because the brain continues to produce dopamine all the time. However, refraining from activities that stem from compulsion and impulse may prove beneficial for short periods of time.

Since many of the activities and substances people turn to can become addictive over time, a bit of distancing from outlets such as social media, fast food, and mindless TV can have an overall positive impact on a person's mind and lifestyle.

Other practices such as meditation may be a far more effective way to achieve a better state of mindfulness, as a "dopamine detox" is not a scientifically proven method, and is at best misleading by definition.

REFERENCES

Links

https://medium.com/swlh/dopamine-fasting-2-0-the-hot-silicon-valley-trend-7c4dc3ba2213

https://www.marieclaire.co.uk/life/health-fitness/dopamine-fasting-680083

https://www.health.harvard.edu/blog/dopamine-fasting-misunderstanding-science-spawns-a-maladaptive-fad-2020022618917

https://www.vox.com/future-perfect/2019/11/13/20959424/dopamine-fasting-silicon-valley-trend-neuroscience

https://www.livescience.com/is-there-science-behind-dopamine-fasting-trend.html
https://thetinylife.com/dopamine-detox-fix-your-brain-and-survive-modern-life-with-a_dopamine-fast/

Journals

Audesirk, T., Audesirk, G., & Byers, B. E. (2008). Biology: Life on earth with physiology. Upper Saddle River, NJ: Pearson Prentice Hall.

Belujon, P., & Grace, A. A. (2017). Dopamine system dysregulation in major depressive disorders. International

Journal of Neuropharmacology, 20(12), 1,036-1,046. doi: 10.1093/ijnp/pyx056

Brisch, R., Saniotis, A., Wolf, R., Bielau, H., Bernstein, H., Steiner, J., Bogerts, B., Braun, K., et al. (2014, May 19). The role of dopamine in schizophrenia from a neurobiological and evolutionary perspective: Old fashioned, but still in vogue. Frontiers in Psychiatry, 5(110). doi: 10.3389/fpsyt.2014.00110

Colman, A. M. (2006). Oxford dictionary of psychology. New York, NY: Oxford University Press.

Diehl, D. J., & Gershon, S. (1992). The role of dopamine in mood disorders. Comprehensive Psychiatry, https://www.sciencedirect.com/science/article/abs/pii/001044 0X9290007D

González S, Moreno-Delgado D, Moreno E, Pérez-Capote K, Franco R, et al. (2012). The role of dopamine in sleep regulation. PLoS Biology, 10(6). doi: 10.1371/journal.pbio.1001347

High dopamine levels: Symptoms & adverse reactions. (n.d.). Mental Health Daily. Retrieved from https://mentalhealthdaily.com/2015/04/01/high-dopamine-leve ls-symptoms-adverse-reactions

Kring, A. M., Johnson, S. L., Davison, G. C., & Neale, J. M. (2010). Abnormal psychology. Hoboken, NJ: John Wiley & Sons.

Love, T., Laier, C., Brand, M., Hatch, L., & Hajela, R. (2015). Neuroscience of internet pornography addiction: A review and update. Behavioral Sciences (Basel),

Mandal, A. (2019, April 9). Dopamine functions. Retrieved from https://www.news-medical.net/health/Dopamine-Functions.aspx

Nieoullon, A. (2002). Dopamine and the regulation of cognition and attention. Progress in Neurobiology, 67(1), 53-83. Retrieved from https://www.ncbi.nlm.nih.gov/pubmed/12126656

The University of California, Neuron